Becoming Like Jesus

Learning from Matthew's Gospel

A Workbook by
James J. Stewart

Copyright © 2025 James J. Stewart

ISBN: 978-1-7362724-8-0

All Biblical quotations are from:
The World English Bible [WEB]
Derived from the *American Standard Version* ©1901
Published by Rainbow Missions, Public Domain (Copyright waived)

> The path of discipleship is narrow, and it is fatally easy to miss one's way and stray from the path, even after years of discipleship. And it's hard t find. On either side of the narrow path deep chasms yawn. To be called to a life of extraordinary quality, to live up to it, and yet to be unconscious of it is indeed a narrow way. To confess and testify to the truth as it is in Jesus, and at the same time to love the enemies of that truth, his enemies and ours, and to love them with the infinite love of Jesus Christ, is indeed a narrow way.
> Dietrich Bonhoeffer

**Becoming More Like Jesus by Learning Discipleship from Matthew's Gospel
as Seen Through the Eyes of the First Century Church**

In this workbook, the emphasis is upon learning more from the Christ of faith and becoming faithful disciples of Jesus. Then, while faithfully following Jesus and trying to be like Him, you can actually become more like Him. Although there are almost always women present when Jesus speaks, Matthew's gospel is focused upon a primarily male audience. Along with the other three canonical gospels, it constitutes the heart of the faith of Christians during those first centuries after Christ's birth. In the years just before Christ's birth, Jews throughout the Roman Empire were praying fervently for the coming of the Messiah [Hebrew] or Christ [Greek]. Matthew testifies to how people responded to the Jesus of history, and how Jesus truly is the promised Messiah.

Introduction

As a spiritual and theological way of seeing Jesus, we can think of our Savior as being the human window through which we can see God. The closer we get to a window, the more we see what's beyond it. Jesus said, "… He who has seen me has seen the Father…." John 14:9b provides us with a glimpse of Jesus' holiness and character. Being a faithful disciple includes both following Jesus and trying to be like Him.

1 Peter 1:15 says, "… but just as he who called you is holy, you yourselves also be holy in all of your behavior…." When we faithfully follow Jesus and try to be like Him, we should have a good attitude towards His holiness and try to be like Him in every way. In the original languages of the Bible, holiness refers to being set apart for God, consecrated, and surrendered to Him as part of being like Him. Spiritually faithful reflection of Jesus means being like Jesus and growing towards our savior's holiness in a practical way. We can observe it at the apostles, and we can attain it in ourselves by striving to be like Him.

The life, death, and resurrection of Jesus, our Savior, is traditionally covered in four books in the New Testament. These four books are located at the start of the New Testament and are known as the Gospels. The word gospel means good news. The New Testament starts with the Gospel of Matthew, followed by that of Mark, Luke, and John. While the Gospels of Matthew, Mark and Luke have numerous parallel passages, the Gospel of John is different. John the Apostle was the youngest of the twelve who were close to Jesus. John's gospel includes more private conversations and fewer accounts of Jesus' public teachings than the gospels of Matthew, Mark, and Luke. This workbook sets up public teachings by Jesus with a simple approach.

1. Read a few verses of the World English Bible that are provided. (You can also use the version or translation you like best.) Notes are provided in this workbook to aid readers in understanding. Similar notes can be found on Annotated Bibles and Study Bibles.
2. These are followed by questions for reflection, prayer, and discussion. There are not necessarily 'good' or 'bad' answers to these questions. They are for thought, consideration, and discussion. The questions help the reader ponder the character and personality of Jesus.

You do not need to have extensive knowledge of the Bible or Jesus to develop your discipleship of Jesus through this book. Small groups have the ability to plan times for discussion that involve everyone in the group.
Reading the Bible regularly can have a significant impact on our lives. Growing and changing spiritually is a result of faithfully following Jesus and attempting to be like Him. While it does not mean necessarily achieve Jesus' holiness, it does mean growing towards faithful discipleship and recognizing His holiness, reflecting it as best we can as we faithfully follow Him and try to be like Him. Use a translation rather than a paraphrase, as a modern paraphrase of the Bible is usually not suitable for serious study or spiritual growth.

The Gospel of Matthew

The Heritage of Jesus: Matthew 1:1-17 [WEB]

The book of the genealogy of Jesus Christ, the son of David, the son of Abraham. 2 Abraham became the father of Isaac. Isaac became the father of Jacob. Jacob became the father of Judah and his brothers. 3 Judah became the father of Perez and Zerah by Tamar. Perez became the father of Hezron. Hezron became the father of Ram. 4 Ram became the father of Amminadab. Amminadab became the father of Nahshon. Nahshon became the father of Salmon. 5 Salmon became the father of Boaz by Rahab. Boaz became the father of Obed by Ruth. Obed became the father of Jesse. 6 Jesse became the father of King David. David the king became the father of Solomon by her who had been Uriah's wife. 7 Solomon became the father of Rehoboam. Rehoboam became the father of Abijah. Abijah became the father of Asa. 8 Asa became the father of Jehoshaphat. Jehoshaphat became the father of Joram. Joram became the father of Uzziah. 9 Uzziah became the father of Jotham. Jotham became the father of Ahaz. Ahaz became the father of Hezekiah. 10 Hezekiah became the father of Manasseh. Manasseh became the father of Amon. Amon became the father of Josiah. 11 Josiah became the father of Jechoniah and his brothers at the time of the exile to Babylon. 12 After the exile to Babylon, Jechoniah became the father of Shealtiel. Shealtiel became the father of Zerubbabel. 13 Zerubbabel became the father of Abiud. Abiud became the father of Eliakim. Eliakim became the father of Azor. 14 Azor became the father of Zadok. Zadok became the father of Achim. Achim became the father of Eliud. 15 Eliud became the father of Eleazar. Eleazar became the father of Matthan. Matthan became the father of Jacob. 16 Jacob became the father of Joseph, the husband of Mary, from whom was born Jesus, who is called Christ. 17 So all the generations from Abraham to David are fourteen generations; from David to the exile to Babylon fourteen generations; and from the carrying away to Babylon to the Christ, fourteen generations.

Compare:
Luke 3:23-38

Notes
1. The origins of Jesus can be traced back to King David and Abraham, the Patriarch of Judaism.
2. Jesus is the first generation in the seventh set of seven generations according to the pattern [17]. The symbolism of the jubilee year, which is scheduled for every 50th year, connects Jesus to the tradition.
3. The pattern was created without the names of Ahaziah, Joash, and Amaziah, which was an accepted practice at the time. The names from Abiud to Jacob are individuals who were not known at the time of the dispersion.
4. Careful records were kept to ensure clean bloodlines and prevent disputes over property.

Questions for Reflection
1. How far back do you trace your ancestors? Is it important to you? Why?

2. How do you understand why this ancestry information was important to Jesus and His siblings?

3. Do you find this information helpful to you as you read the Bible? Why?

Birth & Infancy: Matthew 1:18-25 [WEB]

18 Now the birth of Jesus Christ was like this: After his mother, Mary, was engaged to Joseph, before they came together, she was found pregnant by the Holy Spirit. 19 Joseph, her husband, being a righteous man, and not willing to make her a public example, intended to put her away secretly. 20 But when he thought about these things, behold, an angel of the Lord appeared to him in a dream, saying, "Joseph, son of David, don't be afraid to take to yourself Mary as your wife, for that which is conceived in her is of the Holy Spirit. 21 She shall give birth to a son. You shall name him Jesus, for it is he who shall save his people from their sins." 22 Now all this has happened that it might be fulfilled which was spoken by the Lord through the prophet, saying, 23 "Behold, the virgin shall be with child, and shall give birth to a son. They shall call his name Immanuel," which is, being interpreted, "God with us." 24 Joseph arose from his sleep, and did as the angel of the Lord commanded him, and took his wife to himself; 25 and didn't know her sexually until she had given birth to her firstborn son. He named him Jesus.

Compare:
Luke 1:26-2:40

Notes
1. The name *Jesus* [17] and the phrase *"he will save"* are roughly equivalent in Hebrew and Aramaic.
2. The quotation [23] is from Isaiah 7:14. While Christians see this as a prophecy of the coming of Jesus, those who practice Judaism to this day see it as a prophecy of the coming of King David.

Questions for Reflection
1. Have you ever had a dream that seemed very real after you awakened? If so, describe it.

2. Do you believe God has ever spoken to you through a dream? Again, if so, describe it.

Astrological Visitation: Matthew 2:1-12 [WEB]

Now when Jesus was born in Bethlehem of Judea in the days of King Herod, behold, wise men from the east came to Jerusalem, saying, 2 "Where is he who is born King of the Jews? For we saw his star in the east, and have come to worship him." 3 When King Herod heard it, he was troubled, and all Jerusalem with him. 4 Gathering together all the chief priests and scribes of the people, he asked them where the Christ would be born. 5 They said to him, "In Bethlehem of Judea, for this is written through the prophet, 6 'You Bethlehem, land of Judah, are in no way least among the princes of Judah;for out of you shall come a governor who shall shepherd my people, Israel.'" 7 Then Herod secretly called the wise men, and learned from them exactly what time the star appeared. 8 He sent them to Bethlehem, and said, "Go and search diligently for the young child. When you have found him, bring me word, so that I also may come and worship him." 9 They, having heard the king, went their way; and behold, the star, which they saw in the east, went before them until it came and stood over where the young child was. 10 When they saw the star, they rejoiced with exceedingly great joy. 11 They came into the house and saw the young child with Mary, his mother, and they fell down and worshiped him. Opening their treasures, they offered to him gifts: gold, frankincense, and myrrh. 12 Being warned in a dream not to return to Herod, they went back to their own country another way.

Notes

1. The Magi [*wise men*] were part of both an occupation and class in ancient Persia [Iran]. The stars were a tool for them in the sense that they sought wisdom by pondering them.
2. Herod would see the birth of such a king as a threat to his own children's right to ascendancy to the throne.
3. The actual number of Magi is unknown.

Questions for Reflection

1. Do you understand Astrology to be a harmless pastime, or do you take seriously the Old Testament's prohibition against seeking to know the future in this way?

2. Why do you suppose Matthew includes this story for his Jewish male audience?

3. Why do you think there are still people today who do not want Jesus Christ to be accepted as part of history?

4. If you encounter someone who says Jesus is not historical, how do you respond?

Sojourn in Egypt: Matthew 2:13-23 [WEB]

{13} Now after they had left, an angel of the Lord appeared to Joseph in a dream and said, "Get up, take the child and his mother, and flee to Egypt, and remain there until I tell you; for Herod is about to search for the child, to destroy him." {14} Then Joseph got up, took the child and his mother by night, and went to Egypt, {15} and remained there until the death of Herod. This was to fulfill what had been spoken by the Lord through the prophet, "Out of Egypt I have called my son." {16} When Herod saw that he had been tricked by the wise men, he was infuriated, and he sent and killed all the children in and around Bethlehem who were two years old or under, according to the time that he had learned from the wise men. {17} Then was fulfilled what had been spoken through the prophet Jeremiah: {18} "A voice was heard in Ramah, wailing and loud lamentation, Rachel weeping for her children; she refused to be consoled, because they are no more." {19} When Herod died, an angel of the Lord suddenly appeared in a dream to Joseph in Egypt and said, {20} "Get up, take the child and his mother, and go to the land of Israel, for those who were seeking the child's life are dead." {21} Then Joseph got up, took the child and his mother, and went to the land of Israel. {22} But when he heard that Archelaus was ruling over Judea in place of his father Herod, he was afraid to go there. And after being warned in a dream, he went away to the district of Galilee. {23} There he made his home in a town called Nazareth, so that what had been spoken through the prophets might be fulfilled, "He will be called a Nazorean."

Notes

1. The quotation [18] is from Jeremiah 31:15.
2. Rachel, the wife of Jacob, died in childbirth, and Genesis 35:16-20 indicates she was buried in Bethlehem.
3. ***Rahmah*** was just north of Jerusalem. In Jeremiah 40:1-6 a Babylonian soldier named Nebuzaradan saved Isaiah from harm in the disastrous national defeat of Judah.

Questions for Reflection

1. What impressions do you now have of Joseph, in this limited portrait in the birth narrative?

2. How was Joseph important to Jesus' childhood and developing into an adult?

Jesus Heralded by John: Matthew 3:1-12 [WEB]

In those days, John the Baptizer came, preaching in the wilderness of Judea, saying, 2 "Repent, for the Kingdom of Heaven is at hand!" 3 For this is he who was spoken of by Isaiah the prophet, saying, "The voice of one crying in the wilderness, make the way of the Lord ready! Make his paths straight!" 4 Now John himself wore clothing made of camel's hair with a leather belt around his waist. His food was locusts and wild honey. 5 Then people from Jerusalem, all of Judea, and all the region around the Jordan went out to him. 6 They were baptized by him in the Jordan, confessing their sins. 7 But when he saw many of the Pharisees and Sadducees coming for his baptism, he said to them, "You offspring of vipers, who warned you to flee from the wrath to come? 8 Therefore produce fruit worthy of repentance! 9 Don't think to yourselves, 'We have Abraham for our father,' for I tell you that God is able to raise up children to Abraham from these stones. 10 Even now the ax lies at the root of the trees. Therefore every tree that doesn't produce good fruit is cut down, and cast into the fire. 11 "I indeed baptize you in water for repentance, but he who comes after me is mightier than I, whose sandals I am not worthy to carry. He will baptize you in the Holy Spirit. 12 His winnowing fork is in his hand, and he will thoroughly cleanse his threshing floor. He will gather his wheat into the barn, but the chaff he will burn up with unquenchable fire."

Compare:
Mark 1:1-8
Luke 3:1-18
John 1:6-8, 19-20
Acts 18:25-19:7

Notes
1. John's wilderness activities and speeches were in keeping with traditional accounts of prophets in the Hebrew scriptures.
2. The wilderness of Judea was on the other side of the hills east of Jerusalem, extending southeast to the foot of the Dead Sea.
3. The term **repent** literally means *return* – that is, return to the lifestyle laid out by God's covenant with Israel.
4. The Sadducees and Pharisees formed the two dominant political parties of the time, with the Pharisees being a bit more orthodox or conservative. A third political group, the Essenes, was even more conservative.

Questions for Reflection
1. What are some of today's terms that would be applied to a man like John?

2. What qualities would a man like this have to have for you to respect his teaching?

3. Is the message of John the Baptist appropriate for Christians of today, as well as for Jews? Why?

The Baptism of Jesus: Matthew 3:13-17 [WEB]

13 Then Jesus came from Galilee to the Jordan to John, to be baptized by him. 14 But John would have hindered him, saying, "I need to be baptized by you, and you come to me?" 15 But Jesus, answering, said to him, "Allow it now, for this is the fitting way for us to fulfill all righteousness." Then he allowed him. 16 Jesus, when he was baptized, went up directly from the water: and behold, the heavens were opened to him. He saw the Spirit of God descending as a dove, and coming on him. 17 Behold, a voice out of the heavens said, "This is my beloved Son, with whom I am well pleased."

Compare:
Mark 1:9-11
Luke 3:21-22
John 1:30-34

Notes
1. Previously, baptism was used only for purposes of bonding an individual with a new religion.
2. The passage demonstrates Jesus' respect for John's witness.
3. Jesus was seeking to identify Himself with those who would respond to God's call.

Questions for Reflection
1. Since John undoubtedly knows his cousin, why do you suppose John questions Jesus' desire to be baptized?

2. Does this event mark a change in Jesus, or does it simply mark the beginning of Jesus' earthly ministry?

3. Why does Jesus tell John that His baptism is "necessary?"

4. Do you see all three persons of the Trinity in this passage?

Wilderness Temptations: Matthew 4:1-11 [WEB]

Then Jesus was led up by the Spirit into the wilderness to be tempted by the devil. 2 When he had fasted forty days and forty nights, he was hungry afterward. 3 The tempter came and said to him, "If you are the Son of God, command that these stones become bread." 4 But he answered, "It is written, 'Man shall not live by bread alone, but by every word that proceeds out of God's mouth.' " 5 Then the devil took him into the holy city. He set him on the pinnacle of the temple, 6 and said to him, "If you are the Son of God, throw yourself down, for it is written, 'He will command his angels concerning you,' and, 'On their hands they will bear you up, so that you don't dash your foot against a stone.' " 7 Jesus said to him, "Again, it is written, 'You shall not test the Lord, your God.' " 8 Again, the devil took him to an exceedingly high mountain, and showed him all the kingdoms of the world and their glory. 9 He said to him, "I will give you all of these things, if you will fall down and worship me." 10 Then Jesus said to him, "Get behind me, Satan! For it is written, 'You shall worship the Lord your God, and you shall serve him only.' " 11 Then the devil left him, and behold, angels came and served him.

Compare:
Mark 1:12-13
Luke 4:1-13
Also: Hebrews 2:18 and 4:15

Notes
1. The story of temptation illustrates Jesus' determination to stay focused on the God's mission for Him, without concern about His own safety, logical arguments, or so-called practicality and expediency.
2. His nemesis, who goes by a number of different names, is portrayed as hostile to God's will.

Questions for Reflection
1. With these three temptations serving as illustrations of categories, put own temptations into the same categories, and name some.

2. Does this story make Jesus seem more human or more divine? Why?

3. Do you see any significance to the angels coming to serve Jesus after the temptations? Is it comforting to your own walk of faith? Why?

Jesus Begins Ministry: Matthew 4:12-17 [WEB]

12 Now when Jesus heard that John was delivered up, he withdrew into Galilee. 13 Leaving Nazareth, he came and lived in Capernaum, which is by the sea, in the region of Zebulun and Naphtali, 14 that it might be fulfilled which was spoken through Isaiah the prophet, saying, 15 "The land of Zebulun and the land of Naphtali, toward the sea, beyond the Jordan, Galilee of the Gentiles, 16 the people who sat in darkness saw a great light; to those who sat in the region

and shadow of death, to them light has dawned." 17 From that time, Jesus began to preach, and to say, "Repent! For the Kingdom of Heaven is at hand."

Compare:
Mark 1:14-15
Luke 4:14-15

Notes
1. The arrest of John the Baptist was probably many months after the temptation. Many stories in John's gospel would fit well prior to this event – a very plausible chronology.
2. The quotation is from Isaiah 9:1-2.
3. For Matthew, the phrases ***kingdom of heaven*** and ***kingdom of God*** are synonymous.

Questions for Reflection
1. Is Jesus' opening message similar to that of John the Baptist? For example?

2. Since Jesus opens his public ministry with "Repent! For the Kingdom of Heaven is at hand," what are some ways you can use this as part of the foundation of your faith?

Choosing an Inner Circle: Matthew 4:18-22 [WEB]
18 Walking by the sea of Galilee, he saw two brothers: Simon, who is called Peter, and Andrew, his brother, casting a net into the sea; for they were fishermen. 19 He said to them, "Come after me, and I will make you fishers for men." 20 They immediately left their nets and followed him. 21 Going on from there, he saw two other brothers, James the son of Zebedee, and John his brother, in the boat with Zebedee their father, mending their nets. He called them. 22 They immediately left the boat and their father, and followed him.

Compare:
Mark 1:16-20
Luke 5:1-11
John 1:35-42

Note:
➢ Peter, Andrew, James, and John become a leadership core of the twelve Jesus calls to be His inner circle of disciples.

Questions for Reflection

1. When you became a Christian, did you have a feeling that Jesus was calling you to serve Him? If so, describe it.

2. What do you think are some of the most important ingredients of your life that makes you different from those who are not following Jesus?

First Healings: Matthew 4:23-25 [WEB]

{23} Jesus went throughout Galilee, teaching in their synagogues and proclaiming the good news of the kingdom and curing every disease and every sickness among the people. {24} So his fame spread throughout all Syria, and they brought to him all the sick, those who were afflicted with various diseases and pains, demoniacs, epileptics, and paralytics, and he cured them. {25} And great crowds followed him from Galilee, the Decapolis, Jerusalem, Judea, and from beyond the Jordan.

Note:

➤ With these two verses, Matthew establishes the pattern of ministry that Jesus follows throughout most of His ministry on Earth.

Questions for Reflection

1. Do you see this being taught in your church's preaching and teaching? Give examples.

2. Do you know how today's missionaries do even more? Give examples.

3. Are you involved in reaching out beyond your local church? If so, give examples.

The Beatitudes: Matthew 5:1-12 [WEB]

1 Seeing the multitudes, he went up onto the mountain. When he had sat down, his disciples came to him. 2 He opened his mouth and taught them, saying, 3 "Blessed are the poor in spirit, for theirs is the Kingdom of Heaven. 1, 2 4 Blessed are those who mourn, for they shall be comforted. 1, 2, 3 5 Blessed are the gentle, for they shall inherit the earth. 6 Blessed are those who hunger and thirst after righteousness, for they shall be filled. 7 Blessed are the merciful, for they shall obtain mercy. 8 Blessed are the pure in heart, for they shall see God. 9 Blessed are the peacemakers, for they shall be called children of God. 10 Blessed are those who have been persecuted for righteousness' sake, for theirs is the Kingdom of Heaven. 11 "Blessed are you when people reproach you, persecute you, and say all kinds of evil against you falsely, for my sake. 12 Rejoice, and be exceedingly glad, for great is your reward in heaven. For that is how they persecuted the prophets who were before you.

Compare:
Luke 6:17, 20-23

Notes
1. The Beatitudes communicate the grace of God for those who choose to live under –and with respect for – God's sovereignty.
2. Those who are *poor in spirit* are those with a sense of spiritual humility and destitution.
3. The phrase, *will receive mercy*, seems to indicate future pluperfect – judgment day.
4. Those who are *pure in heart* are more than merely honest, but are transparent in terms of motives.

Questions for Reflection
1. Are there one or more beatitudes that seem to speak directly to who you are right now?

2. What do you suppose is the significance of these sayings for Matthew's Jewish audience typically centered upon the law?

3. As you grow in your faith and become a more faithful disciple, which one of these beatitudes speaks to you the most clearly? Why?

4. If there is a second beatitude that speaks to you clearly, which one? Why?

Evangelism Tools: Matthew 5:13-16 [WEB]

13 "You are the salt of the earth, but if the salt has lost its flavor, with what will it be salted? It is then good for nothing, but to be cast out and trodden under the feet of men. 14 You are the light of the world. A city located on a hill can't be hidden. 15 Neither do you light a lamp, and put it under a measuring basket, but on a stand; and it shines to all who are in the house. 16 Even so, let your light shine before men; that they may see your good works, and glorify your Father who is in heaven.

Compare:
Mark 9:49-50
Luke 14:34-35
John 8:12
Also: Philippians 2:15

Note
- Salt was encrusted on rocks gathered around the shores of the Dead Sea. The rocks were put in a cloth bag that was immersed in a pot to add flavor. Eventually the salt would be dissolved (the 'salt' lost its taste) and the salt-less rocks were discarded.

Questions for Reflection
1. Have you ever had your reserves of faith so low that you that you lost your zest for life? If; so, describe.

2. Are non-churched people aware of the depth of your faith? Describe why or why not.

3. As a student of Jesus and his teachings, what is Jesus saying here that encourages you or discourages you? Why?

Message and Law: Matthew 5:17-20 [WEB]

17 "Don't think that I came to destroy the law or the prophets. I didn't come to destroy, but to fulfill. 18 For most certainly, I tell you, until heaven and earth pass away, not even one smallest letter or one tiny pen stroke shall in any way pass away from the law, until all things are accomplished. 19 Whoever, therefore, shall break one of these least commandments, and teach others to do so, shall be called least in the Kingdom of Heaven; but whoever shall do and teach them shall be called great in the Kingdom of Heaven. 20 For I tell you that unless your righteousness exceeds that of the scribes and Pharisees, there is no way you will enter into the Kingdom of Heaven.

Questions for Reflection
1. Why do you think this passage might be so important to Matthew's Jewish audience focused upon the law?

2. What do you think is the Christian's relationship to the law?

3. As you learn from Jesus and draw closer to him, are you changing your attitude towards the Bible's teachings about the law? How?

Reading Vs. Living Law: Matthew 5:21-30 [WEB]

21 "You have heard that it was said to the ancient ones, 'You shall not murder;' and 'Whoever shall murder shall be in danger of the judgment.' 22 But I tell you, that everyone who is angry with his brother without a cause shall be in danger of the judgment; and whoever shall say to his brother, 'Raca!' shall be in danger of the council; and whoever shall say, 'You fool!' shall be in danger of the fire of Gehenna. 23 "If therefore you are offering your gift at the altar, and there remember that your brother has anything against you, 24 leave your gift there before the altar, and go your way. First be reconciled to your brother, and then come and offer your gift. 25 Agree with your adversary quickly, while you are with him in the way; lest perhaps the prosecutor deliver you to the judge, and the judge deliver you to the officer, and you be cast into prison. 26 Most certainly I tell you, you shall by no means get out of there, until you have paid the last penny. 27 "You have heard that it was said, 'You shall not commit adultery;' 28 but I tell you that everyone who gazes at a woman to lust after her has committed adultery with her already in his heart. 29 If your right eye causes you to stumble, pluck it out and throw it away from you. For it is more profitable for you that one of your members should perish, than for your whole body to be cast into Gehenna. 30 If your right hand causes you to stumble, cut it off, and throw it away from you. For it is more profitable for you that one of your members should perish, than for your whole body to be cast into Gehenna.

Notes
1. Deuteronomy 16:18 provides for a local court in every community.
2. The *council* obviously refers to the Sanhedrin, the local civil governing body.
3. Adultery carried the death penalty.

Questions for Reflection
1. Under these guidelines, when do you think should a Christian use the secular court system?

2. How do these teachings make you feel about your own self-discipline as a Jesus follower?

Marriage Perspective: Matthew 5:31-32 [WEB]

31 "It was also said, 'Whoever shall put away his wife, let him give her a writing of divorce,' 32 but I tell you that whoever puts away his wife, except for the cause of sexual immorality, makes her an adulteress; and whoever marries her when she is put away commits adultery.

Compare:
Mark 10:11-12

Luke 16:18
Also: Romans 7:2-3
Also: 1 Corinthians 7:10-11

Notes
1. Literally translated, the man referred to here is not divorcing his wife but putting her away in a protected and isolated environment so that he can take on another wife. The law specifically provides for divorce and Jesus, as fulfiller of the law is not abolishing divorce.
2. The references to unchastity are absent in both Mark and Luke.

Questions for Reflection
1. Do you believe that the church has historically handled the problems of divorce adequately? Why?

2. Does the church communicate a mixed message regarding divorce in your thinking?

To Tell the Truth: Matthew 5:33-37 [WEB]
33 "Again you have heard that it was said to them of old time, 'You shall not make false vows, but shall perform to the Lord your vows,' 34 but I tell you, don't swear at all: neither by heaven, for it is the throne of God; 35 nor by the earth, for it is the footstool of his feet; nor by Jerusalem, for it is the city of the great King. 36 Neither shall you swear by your head, for you can't make one hair white or black. 37 But let your 'Yes' be 'Yes' and your 'No' be 'No.' Whatever is more than these is of the evil one.

Notes
1. Specifications regarding carrying out vows is found in Leviticus 19:12 and in Deuteronomy 23:21.
2. The Pharisees believed that it was permissible to swear by certain things without penalty.
3. Swearing did not in that culture necessarily mean profanity.

Questions for Reflection
1. Have you ever had to give testimony under oath? If so, how did you feel?

2. Do you ever swear in terms of promising that you are telling the truth?

Grounds for Revenge: Matthew 5:38-42 [WEB]
38 "You have heard that it was said, 'An eye for an eye, and a tooth for a tooth.' 39 But I tell you, don't resist him who is evil; but whoever strikes you on your right cheek, turn to him the other also. 40 If anyone sues you to take away

your coat, let him have your cloak also. 41 Whoever compels you to go one mile, go with him two. 42 Give to him who asks you, and don't turn away him who desires to borrow from you.

Compare:
Exodus 21:23-24
Leviticus 24:19-20
Deuteronomy 19:21

Note
- In primitive society, the idea was to control retaliation rather than try to abolish it. The Torah does not endorse, condone, or justify the practice.

Questions for Reflection
1. Have you ever participated in taking revenge? If so, how do you feel about it now?

2. Why shouldn't a faithful follower of Jesus ever take revenge?

3. Do you see capital punishment as society's taking revenge on the killer? Have you other feelings you can describe?

Love's Proper Context: Matthew 5:43-48 [WEB]
43 "You have heard that it was said, 'You shall love your neighbor, and hate your enemy. 44 But I tell you, love your enemies, bless those who curse you, do good to those who hate you, and pray for those who mistreat you and persecute you, 45 that you may be children of your Father who is in heaven. For he makes his sun to rise on the evil and the good, and sends rain on the just and the unjust. 46 For if you love those who love you, what reward do you have? Don't even the tax collectors do the same? 47 If you only greet your friends, what more do you do than others? Don't even the tax collectors do the same? 48 Therefore you shall be perfect, just as your Father in heaven is perfect.

Compare:
Luke 6:27-28, 32-36

Notes
4. Since children model their behavior after that of their parents, the phrase **children of God** is understood to means trying to make one's attitudes and character modeled after that of God.
5. The command is to **be perfect** in one's love for all. **Perfect**, a translation of the Greek word *teleios* means complete at that point in such things as labor, growth and character.

Question for Reflection

- Are there people that you love conditionally? What does that mean for you?

An Attitude of Piety: Matthew 6:1-4 [WEB]

1 "Be careful that you don't do your charitable giving before men, to be seen by them, or else you have no reward from your Father who is in heaven. 2 Therefore when you do merciful deeds, don't sound a trumpet before yourself, as the hypocrites do in the synagogues and in the streets, that they may get glory from men. Most certainly I tell you, they have received their reward. 3 But when you do merciful deeds, don't let your left hand know what your right hand does, 4 so that your merciful deeds may be in secret, then your Father who sees in secret will reward you openly.

Compare:
Luke 18:10-14

Notes
1. In that world, giving alms was the ultimate act of public piety.
2. The comparison is between instant gratification – the reward of this world –, or the pleasure of God – with reward in life eternal.

Questions for Reflection
1. Do you like getting credit from others for the things you do for God?

2. Are volunteers you know more likely to do more if they get recognition for their work?

3. How might Matthew's Jewish audience receive this teaching, based upon what you know of the culture of Jesus' time?

Effective Prayer: Matthew 6:5-15 [WEB]

5 "When you pray, you shall not be as the hypocrites, for they love to stand and pray in the synagogues and in the corners of the streets, that they may be seen by men. Most certainly, I tell you, they have received their reward. 6 But you, when you pray, enter into your inner room, and having shut your door, pray to your Father who is in secret, and your Father who sees in secret will reward you openly. 7 In praying, don't use vain repetitions, as the Gentiles do; for they think that they will be heard for their much speaking. 8 Therefore don't be like them, for your Father knows what things you need, before you ask him. 9 Pray like this: 'Our Father in heaven, may your name be kept holy. 10 Let your Kingdom come. Let your will be done, as in heaven, so on earth. 11 Give us today our daily bread. 12 Forgive us our debts, as we also forgive our debtors. 13 Bring us not into temptation, but deliver us from the evil one. For yours is the Kingdom, the power, and the glory forever. Amen.' 14 "For if you forgive men their trespasses, your heavenly Father will also forgive you. 15 But if you don't forgive men their trespasses, neither will your Father forgive your trespasses.

Compare:
Luke 11:2-4
1 Chronicles 29:11-13

Notes
1. The Greek seems to indicate that ***on earth as it is in heaven*** applies to all three of the first petitions. [9-10]
2. In the liturgy of the early church, a concluding expression of praise, as in David's prayer (1 Chronicles), was added at the end of Jesus' teaching.
3. Jesus says to pray *'like this,'* or, follow this pattern.

Questions for Reflection
1. Do you try to follow the pattern of the Lord's prayer as you understand it as at least part of your times of prayer?

2. Are there other patterns that you sometimes follow as part of your conversations with God?

Rewards of Fasting: Matthew 6:16-18 [WEB]
16 "Moreover when you fast, don't be like the hypocrites, with sad faces. For they disfigure their faces, that they may be seen by men to be fasting. Most certainly I tell you, they have received their reward. 17 But you, when you fast, anoint your head, and wash your face; 18 so that you are not seen by men to be fasting, but by your Father who is in secret, and your Father, who sees in secret, will reward you.

Notes
1. Regular fasting was seen as an act of piety.
2. Fasting seldom excluded eating and drinking totally. Rather, it usually meant giving up most if not all solid food.

Questions for Reflection
1. Do you believe that fasting is spiritually helpful for you? If so, how long have you fasted?

2. Are there things you would be willing to do as acts of piety instead of fasting?

Utilizing Treasure: Matthew 6:19-21 [WEB]
19 "Don't lay up treasures for yourselves on the earth, where moth and rust consume, and where thieves break through and steal; 20 but lay up for yourselves treasures in heaven, where neither moth nor rust consume, and where thieves don't break through and steal; 21 for where your treasure is, there your heart will be also.

Compare:
James 5:2-3

Note
- In the ancient world, wealth was often accumulated in expensive clothing and tapestries.

Questions for Reflection
1. Do you consider yourself a good steward, not only in terms of your money, but in terms of all that God has provided for you?

2. Do you believe that part of being faithful to God is being a tither and a good steward in general? Why?

3. How much of your possessions would you **not** grieve over if there were a disaster?

4. Do you think there are there differences today between the ways Jews and Christians value worldly possessions?

Values Lessons: Matthew 6:22-24 [WEB]
22 "The lamp of the body is the eye. If therefore your eye is sound, your whole body will be full of light. 23 But if your eye is evil, your whole body will be full of darkness. If therefore the light that is in you is darkness, how great is the darkness! 24 "No one can serve two masters, for either he will hate the one and love the other; or else he will be devoted to one and despise the other. You can't serve both God and Mammon.

Compare:
Luke 11:34-36; 16:13

Question for Reflection
1. What or who in this world do you value the most?

2. How are values reshaping the political landscape in your world?

About Anxiety: Matthew 6:25-34 [WEB]

25 Therefore I tell you, don't be anxious for your life: what you will eat, or what you will drink; nor yet for your body, what you will wear. Isn't life more than food, and the body more than clothing? 26 See the birds of the sky, that they don't sow, neither do they reap, nor gather into barns. Your heavenly Father feeds them. Aren't you of much more value than they? 27 "Which of you, by being anxious, can add one moment to his lifespan? 28 Why are you anxious about clothing? Consider the lilies of the field, how they grow. They don't toil, neither do they spin, 29 yet I tell you that even Solomon in all his glory was not dressed like one of these. 30 But if God so clothes the grass of the field, which today exists, and tomorrow is thrown into the oven, won't he much more clothe you, you of little faith? 31 "Therefore don't be anxious, saying, 'What will we eat?', 'What will we drink?' or, 'With what will we be clothed?' 32 For the Gentiles seek after all these things; for your heavenly Father knows that you need all these things. 33 But seek first God's Kingdom, and his righteousness; and all these things will be given to you as well. 34 Therefore don't be anxious for tomorrow, for tomorrow will be anxious for itself. Each day's own evil is sufficient.

Compare:
Luke 12:22-31

Notes
1. Those with little faith are unwilling to trust God with all the cares of their lives.
2. Being anxious or worrying should not be confused with normal human concern.

Questions for Reflection
1. What are the things that concern you the most? Do you worry about them? Why

2. Have you ever prayed about something enough that you were able to totally surrender it to God?

3. Knowing that God is all that is good, are you able to trust God thank Him for His answer, even before you see His answer? Why?

Judgment of Others: Matthew 7:1-6 [WEB]

1 "Don't judge, so that you won't be judged. 2 For with whatever judgment you judge, you will be judged; and with whatever measure you measure, it will be measured to you. 3 Why do you see the speck that is in your brother's eye, but don't consider the beam that is in your own eye? 4 Or how will you tell your brother, 'Let me remove the speck from your eye;' and behold, the beam is in your own eye? 5 You hypocrite! First remove the beam out of your own eye, and then you can see clearly to remove the speck out of your brother's eye. 6 "Don't give that which is holy to the dogs, neither throw your pearls before the pigs, lest perhaps they trample them under their feet, and turn and tear you to pieces.

Compare:
Luke 6:37-38, 41-42
Mark 4:24

Notes
1. Jesus proscribes us from judging others in areas where we do not wish to be judged.
2. Meat resulting from sacrifice in the Temple was considered holy.
3. In Greek there are two words for **dogs**, One refers to household pets, and the other refers to the wild dogs that inhabited the garbage dump outside the city [Hell]. Giving what is holy to either would be inappropriate.

Questions for Reflection
1. Are there areas where you feel comfortable making judgment calls? If so, give examples.

2. What are some important areas where you must be careful about making a judgment call?

God's Grace to Golden Rule: Matthew 7:7-14 [WEB]

7 "Ask, and it will be given you. Seek, and you will find. Knock, and it will be opened for you. 8 For everyone who asks receives. He who seeks finds. To him who knocks it will be opened. 9 Or who is there among you, who, if his son asks him for bread, will give him a stone? 10 Or if he asks for a fish, who will give him a serpent? 11 If you then, being evil, know how to give good gifts to your children, how much more will your Father who is in heaven give good things to those who ask him! 12 Therefore whatever you desire for men to do to you, you shall also do to them; for this is the law and the prophets. 13 "Enter in by the narrow gate; for wide is the gate and broad is the way that leads to destruction, and many are those who enter in by it. 14 How narrow is the gate, and restricted is the way that leads to life! Few are those who find it.

Compare:
Mark 11:23-24
John 15:7, 16
1 John 3:21-22 & 5:14-15

Questions for Reflection

1. Are **asking, seeking, and knocking** a sequence, or do you see them as separate ways of seeking God and God's will? Why?

2. Do you believe that faith in God requires this simple approach, or are things more complicated in terms of making our requests of God? Describe your approach.

3. Do you think these verses reflect the Golden Rule? Why?

4. Do you think the teaching about the **narrow gate** is an extension of the Golden Rule? Why?

False and True Prophets: Matthew 7:15-23 [WEB]

15 "Beware of false prophets, who come to you in sheep's clothing, but inwardly are ravening wolves. 16 By their fruits you will know them. Do you gather grapes from thorns, or figs from thistles? 17 Even so, every good tree produces good fruit; but the corrupt tree produces evil fruit. 18 A good tree can't produce evil fruit, neither can a corrupt tree produce good fruit. 19 Every tree that doesn't grow good fruit is cut down, and thrown into the fire. 20 Therefore by their fruits you will know them. 21 Not everyone who says to me, 'Lord, Lord,' will enter into the Kingdom of Heaven; but he who does the will of my Father who is in heaven. 22 Many will tell me in that day, 'Lord, Lord, didn't we prophesy in your name, in your name cast out demons, and in your name do many mighty works?' 23 Then I will tell them, 'I never knew you. Depart from me, you who work iniquity.'

Compare:
Luke 6:43-45

Notes

1. In essence, a prophet is someone who at times sees things from God's perspective. This seldom means fortune telling of a psychic variety.
2. Jesus' no-nonsense approach for discriminating between prophets seems obvious to us in hindsight, but in its time was quite prophetic of itself.
3. Performing seemingly miraculous things does not necessarily denote a prophet.

Questions for Reflection

1. Have you known any people with reasonably good track records in terms of prophecy? If so, describe.

2. Does this help you grow in your understanding of Jesus and his teachings? How?

Listening: Matthew 7:24-29 [WEB]

24 "Everyone therefore who hears these words of mine, and does them, I will liken him to a wise man, who built his house on a rock. 25 The rain came down, the floods came, and the winds blew, and beat on that house; and it didn't fall, for it was founded on the rock. 26 Everyone who hears these words of mine, and doesn't do them will be like a foolish man, who built his house on the sand. 27 The rain came down, the floods came, and the winds blew, and beat on that house; and it fell—and great was its fall." 28 It happened, when Jesus had finished saying these things, that the multitudes were astonished at his teaching, 29 for he taught them with authority, and not like the scribes.

Compare:
Luke 6:47-49
James 1:22-25

Notes
1. Once again, Jesus offers a very pragmatic, down to earth illustration to make his point.
2. The expression, **when Jesus had finished** is used throughout Matthew's gospel when he concludes the five major discourses used in his testimony.

Questions for Reflection
1. Does this sermon [chapters 5-7] seem like one continuous sermon, or does it seem like a collection of highlights of his teachings? Why?

2. Does a major section of teachings like this help you understand his teachings more completely? Explain.

3. Do these teachings help you grow closer in your sense of belonging to Jesus?

Journey to Capernaum: Matthew 8:1-4 [WEB]

1 When he came down from the mountain, great multitudes followed him. 2 Behold, a leper came to him and worshiped him, saying, "Lord, if you want to, you can make me clean." 3 Jesus stretched out his hand, and touched him, saying, "I want to. Be made clean." Immediately his leprosy was cleansed. 4 Jesus said to him, "See that you tell nobody, but go, show yourself to the priest, and offer the gift that Moses commanded, as a testimony to them."

Compare:
Mark 1:40-44
Luke 5:12-14

Notes
1. Skin diseases, usually denoted as **leprosy**, excluded the sufferer from fellowship with the rest of the community.
2. The healer often had to touch the one afflicted, which would make them unclean until certified as clean by a priest. Someone else under other circumstances would thus consider the action of Jesus risky.
3. While most of Matthew's gospel is focused upon Jesus' public teachings to crowds, this is the beginning of an interlude.

Questions for Reflection
1. Have you ever experienced spontaneous healing? If so, describe it.

2. Have you ever sought healing in the context of the whole church, from the elders, or from the pastor? If so, describe

Acts of Compassion: Matthew 8:5-13 [WEB]

5 When he came into Capernaum, a centurion came to him, asking him, 6 and saying, "Lord, my servant lies in the house paralyzed, grievously tormented." 7 Jesus said to him, "I will come and heal him." 8 The centurion answered, "Lord, I'm not worthy for you to come under my roof. Just say the word, and my servant will be healed. 9 For I am also a man under authority, having under myself soldiers. I tell this one, 'Go,' and he goes; and tell another, 'Come,' and he comes; and tell my servant, 'Do this,' and he does it." 10 When Jesus heard it, he marveled, and said to those who followed, "Most certainly I tell you, I haven't found so great a faith, not even in Israel. 11 I tell you that many will come from the east and the west, and will sit down with Abraham, Isaac, and Jacob in the Kingdom of Heaven, 12 but the children of the Kingdom will be thrown out into the outer darkness. There will be weeping and gnashing of teeth." 13 Jesus said to the centurion, "Go your way. Let it be done for you as you have believed." His servant was healed in that hour.

Compare:
Luke 7:1-10
John 4:46-53

Notes
1. A *centurion* was a Roman Army officer who had charge of 50 to 100 men.
2. Believing that Jesus is the Son of God, the centurion believes that Jesus has authority and/or power over disease-causing demons in the same way that he has authority over his men.

Questions for Reflection
1. Do you believe that Jesus has authority and/or power over diseases? Explain this belief for yourself.

2. Do you trust God unconditionally, trusting him to do what is best for someone, even if it is not what you want? Why?

3. Do you ever call upon Jesus for healing for yourself, trusting Him with all that you are and have with the full belief that he has the authority to heal? What has been the result?

Healing Peter's mother-in-law: Matthew 8:14-17 [WEB]
14 When Jesus came into Peter's house, he saw his wife's mother lying sick with a fever. 15 He touched her hand, and the fever left her. She got up and served him. 16 When evening came, they brought to him many possessed with demons. He cast out the spirits with a word, and healed all who were sick; 17 that it might be fulfilled which was spoken through Isaiah the prophet, saying: "He took our infirmities, and bore our diseases."

Compare:
Mark 1:29-34
Luke 4:38-41

Questions for Reflection
1. Do you believe there is a difference between faith healing and spiritual healing? Explain any difference.

2. Do you believe that the healing of Peter's mother-in-law was based upon her belief or His action? Why?

3. Ask yourself the same question regarding the others who were sick, and describe what you believe.

Two Types of Followers: Matthew 8:18-22 [WEB]

18 Now when Jesus saw great multitudes around him, he gave the order to depart to the other side. 19 A scribe came, and said to him, "Teacher, I will follow you wherever you go." 20 Jesus said to him, "The foxes have holes, and the birds of the sky have nests, but the Son of Man has nowhere to lay his head." 21 Another of his disciples said to him, "Lord, allow me first to go and bury my father." 22 But Jesus said to him, "Follow me, and leave the dead to bury their own dead."

Compare:
Mark 4:35
Luke 8:22
Luke 9:57-60

Notes
1. In the gospels of Matthew, Mark, and Luke – Son of Man is a common self-designation by Jesus.
2. The command to *follow me* is grammatically imperative, meaning that Jesus' call must take precedence over everything else.

Question for Reflection
➢ Of these the scribe and the other disciple, which person do you identify with the most? Why?

A Storm on the Sea: Matthew 8:23-27 [WEB]

23 When he got into a boat, his disciples followed him. 24 Behold, a violent storm came up on the sea, so much that the boat was covered with the waves, but he was asleep. 25 They came to him, and woke him up, saying, "Save us, Lord! We are dying!" 26 He said to them, "Why are you fearful, O you of little faith?" Then he got up, rebuked the wind and the sea, and there was a great calm. 27 The men marveled, saying, "What kind of man is this, that even the wind and the sea obey him?"

Compare:
Mark 4:36-41
Luke 8:22-24

Questions for Reflection
1. If Jesus was so lacking in fear that he went to sleep, why do you think the disciples react as they did?

2. Why do you suppose Matthew includes this story in his gospel?

3. At this point in your spiritual growth, would you be afraid as those in the boat were? Why?

Confronting Demons: Mathew 8:28-34 [WEB]

28 When he came to the other side, into the country of the Gergesenes, two people possessed by demons met him there, coming out of the tombs, exceedingly fierce, so that nobody could pass that way. 29 Behold, they cried out, saying, "What do we have to do with you, Jesus, Son of God? Have you come here to torment us before the time?" 30 Now there was a herd of many pigs feeding far away from them. 31 The demons begged him, saying, "If you cast us out, permit us to go away into the herd of pigs." 32 He said to them, "Go!" They came out, and went into the herd of pigs: and behold, the whole herd of pigs rushed down the cliff into the sea, and died in the water. 33 Those who fed them fled, and went away into the city, and told everything, including what happened to those who were possessed with demons. 34 Behold, all the city came out to meet Jesus. When they saw him, they begged that he would depart from their borders.

Compare:
Mark 5:1-20
Luke 8:26-39

Notes
1. The number of people that Jesus heals in this instance is not a major issue, but rather the demon possession.
2. Evidently this occurs in the region of Perea near Gadara, the capital.

Questions for Reflection
1. Have you ever been in the presence of someone who is out of touch with reality? Were you afraid? Please describe.

2. Under what conditions would you be willing to minister to the needs of someone like this?

Healing a Paralytic: Matthew 9:1-8 [WEB]

1 He entered into a boat, and crossed over, and came into his own city. 2 Behold, they brought to him a man who was paralyzed, lying on a bed. Jesus, seeing their faith, said to the paralytic, "Son, cheer up! Your sins are forgiven you." 3 Behold, some of the scribes said to themselves, "This man blasphemes." 4 Jesus, knowing their thoughts, said, "Why do you think evil in your hearts? 5 For which is easier, to say, 'Your sins are forgiven;' or to say, 'Get up, and walk?' 6 But that you may know that the Son of Man has authority on earth to forgive sins..." (then he said to the paralytic), "Get up, and take up your mat, and go up to your house." 7 He arose and departed to his house. 8 But when the multitudes saw it, they marveled and glorified God, who had given such authority to men.

Compare:
Mark 2:1-12
Luke 5:17-26

Notes
1. Since Jesus had made Capernaum His base of operations in Galilee, it was considered ***his own town***.
2. Since he believed his sins were forgiven, he also believed he was healed, and his faith healed him.

Dinner with a Sinner: Matthew 9:9-13 [WEB]

9 As Jesus passed by from there, he saw a man called Matthew sitting at the tax collection office. He said to him, "Follow me." He got up and followed him. 10 It happened as he sat in the house, behold, many tax collectors and sinners came and sat down with Jesus and his disciples. 11 When the Pharisees saw it, they said to his disciples, "Why does your teacher eat with tax collectors and sinners?" 12 When Jesus heard it, he said to them, "Those who are healthy have no need for a physician, but those who are sick do. 13 But you go and learn what this means: 'I desire mercy, and not sacrifice,' for I came not to call the righteous, but sinners to repentance."

Compare:
Mark 2:13-17
Luke 5:27-32

Note
➢ The reader usually assumes that the house was Matthew's.

Questions for Reflection
1. Is it important that people be together as the church with the spiritual presence of Christ? Why?

2. What are some things that can happen when people gather as the church seeking and finding the presence of Christ?

John's Disciples Seeking: Matthew 9:14-17 [WEB]

14 Then John's disciples came to him, saying, "Why do we and the Pharisees fast often, but your disciples don't fast?" 15 Jesus said to them, "Can the friends of the bridegroom mourn, as long as the bridegroom is with them? But the days will come when the bridegroom will be taken away from them, and then they will fast. 16 No one puts a piece of unshrunk cloth on an old garment; for the patch would tear away from the garment, and a worse hole is made. 17 Neither do people put new wine into old wineskins, or else the skins would burst, and the wine be spilled, and the skins ruined. No, they put new wine into fresh wineskins, and both are preserved."

Compare:
Mark 2:18-22
Luke 5:33-39

Notes
1. The frequency of fasting is not the issue. Some manuscripts do not use the term **often** for John's disciples' fasting.
2. The cloth and wineskin analogies illustrate the inappropriateness of comparing the two ministries.

Questions for Reflection
1. Do you believe that the "bridegroom" is part of your church family?

2. Do you believe you can use fasting as one of your spiritual disciplines? Why?

Resurrection or Healing: Matthew 9:18-26 [WEB]
18 While he told these things to them, behold, a ruler came and worshiped him, saying, "My daughter has just died, but come and lay your hand on her, and she will live." 19 Jesus got up and followed him, as did his disciples. 20 Behold, a woman who had an issue of blood for twelve years came behind him, and touched the fringe of his garment; 21 for she said within herself, "If I just touch his garment, I will be made well." 22 But Jesus, turning around and seeing her, said, "Daughter, cheer up! Your faith has made you well." And the woman was made well from that hour. 23 When Jesus came into the ruler's house, and saw the flute players, and the crowd in noisy disorder, 24 he said to them, "Make room, because the girl isn't dead, but sleeping." They were ridiculing him. 25 But when the crowd was put out, he entered in, took her by the hand, and the girl arose. 26 The report of this went out into all that land.

Compare:
Mark 5:21-43
Luke 8:40-56

Notes
1. The Greek verb translated **be made well** implies rescue from imminent ruin or rescue from an overwhelming power.
2. The musicians were hired to professionally mourn the death of the girl.
3. Greek manuscripts lack the specification that the leader was from the synagogue.
4. This account does not identify either the father or the daughter by name.

Questions for Reflection

1. Why do you think this story was of interest to Matthew's Jewish audience?

2. As a student and follower of Jesus, what are some of the things you learn in this passage?

3. As you read this passage, do you feel closer to Jesus? Why?

Healing Two Blind Men: Matthew 9:27-31 [WEB]

27 As Jesus passed by from there, two blind men followed him, calling out and saying, "Have mercy on us, son of David!" 28 When he had come into the house, the blind men came to him. Jesus said to them, "Do you believe that I am able to do this?" They told him, "Yes, Lord." 29 Then he touched their eyes, saying, "According to your faith be it done to you." 30 Their eyes were opened. Jesus strictly commanded them, saying, "See that no one knows about this." 31 But they went out and spread abroad his fame in all that land.

Questions for Reflection

1. Why do you think Jesus said that their healing was according to their faith?

2. Do you think Jesus used reverse psychology when He ordered them not to spread the news of their healing?

Further Healings: Matthew 9:32-38 [WEB]

32 As they went out, behold, a mute man who was demon possessed was brought to him. 33 When the demon was cast out, the mute man spoke. The multitudes marveled, saying, "Nothing like this has ever been seen in Israel!" 34 But the Pharisees said, "By the prince of the demons, he casts out demons." 35 Jesus went about all the cities and the villages, teaching in their synagogues, and preaching the Good News of the Kingdom, and healing every disease and every sickness among the people. 36 But when he saw the multitudes, he was moved with compassion for them, because they were harassed and scattered, like sheep without a shepherd. 37 Then he said to his disciples, "The harvest indeed is plentiful, but the laborers are few. 38 Pray therefore that the Lord of the harvest will send out laborers into his harvest."

Questions for Reflection

1. What do you think is the harvest that Jesus is talking about?

2. Why do you suppose Matthew emphasizes that Jesus healed *every* disease and sickness?

Jesus Sends His Disciples Out: Matthew 10:1-4 [WEB]

1 He called to himself his twelve disciples, and gave them authority over unclean spirits, to cast them out, and to heal every disease and every sickness. 2 Now the names of the twelve apostles are these. The first, Simon, who is called Peter; Andrew, his brother; James the son of Zebedee; John, his brother; 3 Philip; Bartholomew; Thomas; Matthew the tax collector; James the son of Alphaeus; Lebbaeus, whose surname was Thaddaeus; 4 Simon the Canaanite; and Judas Iscariot, who also betrayed him.

Question for Reflection

- Do you think Christians today have the same kind of spiritual authority that Jesus gave to the twelve here? Why do you think so?

Ministry Instructions: Matthew 10:5-15 [WEB]

5 Jesus sent these twelve out, and commanded them, saying, "Don't go among the Gentiles, and don't enter into any city of the Samaritans. 6 Rather, go to the lost sheep of the house of Israel. 7 As you go, preach, saying, 'The Kingdom of Heaven is at hand!' 8 Heal the sick, cleanse the lepers, and cast out demons. Freely you received, so freely give. 9 Don't take any gold, nor silver, nor brass in your money belts. 10 Take no bag for your journey, neither two coats, nor shoes, nor staff: for the laborer is worthy of his food. 11 Into whatever city or village you enter, find out who in it is worthy; and stay there until you go on. 12 As you enter into the household, greet it. 13 If the household is worthy, let your peace come on it, but if it isn't worthy, let your peace return to you. 14 Whoever doesn't receive you, nor hear your words, as you go out of that house or that city, shake off the dust from your feet. 15 Most certainly I tell you, it will be more tolerable for the land of Sodom and Gomorrah in the day of judgment than for that city.

Compare:
Mark 6:8-11,
Luke 9:2-5
Luke 10:3-12
Luke 22:35-38

Notes
1. The instructions imply that only through acceptance of the message and of the messenger could healing occur.
2. Eternal life comes to those who respond positively to the message.

Questions for Reflection
1. How would you feel with proceeding with serving God after receiving these instructions from Jesus? Would you feel afraid? Why?

2. Do you believe that this kind of ministry is going on anywhere today? Why?

Rejection Warning: Matthew 10:16-23 [WEB]

16 "Behold, I send you out as sheep in the midst of wolves. Therefore be wise as serpents, and harmless as doves. 17 But beware of men: for they will deliver you up to councils, and in their synagogues they will scourge you. 18 Yes, and you will be brought before governors and kings for my sake, for a testimony to them and to the nations. 19 But when they deliver you up, don't be anxious how or what you will say, for it will be given you in that hour what you will say. 20 For it is not you who speak, but the Spirit of your Father who speaks in you. 21 "Brother will deliver up brother to death, and the father his child. Children will rise up against parents, and cause them to be put to death. 22 You will be hated by all men for my name's sake, but he who endures to the end will be saved. 23 But when they persecute you in this city, flee into the next, for most certainly I tell you, you will not have gone through the cities of Israel, until the Son of Man has come.

Compare:
Mark 13:9-13
Luke 21:12-17

Note
➢ Jesus' name [22] in His culture referred His identity, His power, and His message.

Questions for Reflection
1. Are there places in the world today where this warning should be applied? Where?

2. Have you ever experienced any hostility to your being a Christian? If so, give an example.

3. If you ever experience hostility to your being a follower of Jesus, do you think you will be able to stand firm in your faith? Why?

Ministry in Perspective: Matthew 10:24-42 [WEB]
24 "A disciple is not above his teacher, nor a servant above his lord. 25 It is enough for the disciple that he be like his teacher, and the servant like his lord. If they have called the master of the house Beelzebul, how much more those of his household! 26 Therefore don't be afraid of them, for there is nothing covered that will not be revealed; and hidden that will not be known. 27 What I tell you in the darkness, speak in the light; and what you hear whispered in the ear, proclaim on the housetops. 28 Don't be afraid of those who kill the body, but are not able to kill the soul. Rather, fear him who is able to destroy both soul and body in Gehenna. 29 "Aren't two sparrows sold for an assarion coin? Not one of them falls on the ground apart from your Father's will, 30 but the very hairs of your head are all numbered. 31 Therefore don't be afraid. You are of more value than many sparrows. 32 Everyone therefore who confesses me before men, him I will also confess before my Father who is in heaven. 33 But whoever denies me before men, him I will also deny before my Father who is in heaven. 34 "Don't think that I came to send peace on the earth. I didn't come to send peace, but a sword. 35 For I came to set a man at odds against his father, and a daughter against her mother, and a daughter-in-law against her mother-in-law. 36 A man's foes will be those of his own household. 37 He who loves father or mother more than me is not worthy of me; and he who loves son or daughter more than me isn't worthy of me. 38 He who doesn't take his cross and follow after me, isn't worthy of me. 39 He who seeks his life will lose it; and he who

loses his life for my sake will find it. 40 He who receives you receives me, and he who receives me receives him who sent me. 41 He who receives a prophet in the name of a prophet will receive a prophet's reward. He who receives a righteous man in the name of a righteous man will receive a righteous man's reward. 42 Whoever gives one of these little ones just a cup of cold water to drink in the name of a disciple, most certainly I tell you he will in no way lose his reward."

Note
- Jesus' instruction to proclaim the good news from the housetops is in stark contrast to the practice of the Essenes, a group of Jews that had all kinds of secret internal doctrines.

Questions for Reflection
1. Do you think that any of these prophecies are being fulfilled anywhere today? Explain why you think so.

2. Do you believe you will experience any of these things during your lifetime, where you will have to face negative consequences because you follow Jesus?

3. If this happens, do you think you will stand firm and trust Jesus under all circumstances? Why?

Jesus Discusses John: Matthew 11:1-15 [WEB]

1 It happened that when Jesus had finished directing his twelve disciples, he departed from there to teach and preach in their cities. 2 Now when John heard in the prison the works of Christ, he sent two of his disciples 3 and said to him, "Are you he who comes, or should we look for another?" 4 Jesus answered them, "Go and tell John the things which you hear and see: 5 the blind receive their sight, the lame walk, the lepers are cleansed, the deaf hear, the dead are raised up, and the poor have good news preached to them. 6 Blessed is he who finds no occasion for stumbling in me." 7 As these went their way, Jesus began to say to the multitudes concerning John, "What did you go out into the wilderness to see? A reed shaken by the wind? 8 But what did you go out to see? A man in soft clothing? Behold, those who wear soft clothing are in king's houses. 9 But why did you go out? To see a prophet? Yes, I tell you, and much more than a prophet. 10 For this is he, of whom it is written, 'Behold, I send my messenger before your face, who will prepare your way before you.' 11 Most certainly I tell you, among those who are born of women there has not arisen anyone greater than John the Baptizer; yet he who is least in the Kingdom of Heaven is greater than he. 12 From the days of John the Baptizer until now, the Kingdom of Heaven suffers violence, and the violent take it by force. 13 For all the prophets and the law prophesied until John. 14 If you are willing to receive it, this is Elijah, who is to come. 15 He who has ears to hear, let him hear.

Compare:
Luke 7:18-35

Notes
1. John's imprisonment was probably at Machaerus, a fortress about five miles east of the Dead Sea.
2. In this rhetoric between Jesus and John, Jesus suggests John answer his own question [6].
3. The quotation [10] is from Malachi 3:1.

Questions for Reflection
1. Does Jesus seem to expect the literal return of Elijah? Explain why you think so.

2. Since John recognized Jesus at His baptism, why do you think John sent two of his disciples to Jesus with that question?

3. Of all the things Jesus said in this passage, what seems the most important to you?

Current Generation: Matthew 11:16-24 [WEB]

16 "But to what shall I compare this generation? It is like children sitting in the marketplaces, who call to their companions 17 and say, 'We played the flute for you, and you didn't dance. We mourned for you, and you didn't lament.' 18 For John came neither eating nor drinking, and they say, 'He has a demon.' 19 The Son of Man came eating and drinking, and they say, 'Behold, a gluttonous man and a drunkard, a friend of tax collectors and sinners!' But wisdom is justified by her children." 20 Then he began to denounce the cities in which most of his mighty works had been done, because they didn't repent. 21 "Woe to you, Chorazin! Woe to you, Bethsaida! For if the mighty works had

been done in Tyre and Sidon which were done in you, they would have repented long ago in sackcloth and ashes. 22 But I tell you, it will be more tolerable for Tyre and Sidon on the day of judgment than for you. 23 You, Capernaum, who are exalted to heaven, you will go down to Hades. For if the mighty works had been done in Sodom which were done in you, it would have remained until this day. 24 But I tell you that it will be more tolerable for the land of Sodom, on the day of judgment, than for you."

Notes

1. With subtle humor, Jesus indicates that there is no pleasing those wrapped up too seriously in their own personal religion. They criticized John for his denial of earthly pleasures, and they criticized Jesus for embracing those same pleasures.
2. The towns mentioned were north of Capernaum. Chorazin was a little over two miles north, and Bethsaida was at the northern end of the Sea of Galilee.

Questions for Reflection

1. Explain your understanding the importance of repentance.

2. Have you ever found yourself defending a position, where you were debating a person who could not be satisfied with your arguments? Explain why you did.

Call to Discipleship: Matthew 11:25-30 [WEB]

25 At that time, Jesus answered, "I thank you, Father, Lord of heaven and earth, that you hid these things from the wise and understanding, and revealed them to infants. 26 Yes, Father, for so it was well-pleasing in your sight. 27 All things have been delivered to me by my Father. No one knows the Son, except the Father; neither does anyone know the Father, except the Son, and he to whom the Son desires to reveal him. 28 "Come to me, all you who labor and are heavily burdened, and I will give you rest. 29 Take my yoke upon you, and learn from me, for I am gentle and lowly in heart; and you will find rest for your souls. 30 For my yoke is easy, and my burden is light."

Compare:
Luke 10:21-22

Question for Reflection

➤ Does this prayer say anything to you personally or about anyone you know? Describe this prayer's meaning for you.

Violating the Sabbath: Matthew 12:1-14 [WEB]

1 At that time, Jesus went on the Sabbath day through the grain fields. His disciples were hungry and began to pluck heads of grain and to eat. 2 But the Pharisees, when they saw it, said to him, "Behold, your disciples do what is not lawful to do on the Sabbath." 3 But he said to them, "Haven't you read what David did, when he was hungry, and those who were with him; 4 how he entered into God's house, and ate the show bread, which was not lawful for him to eat, neither for those who were with him, but only for the priests? 5 Or have you not read in the law, that on the Sabbath day, the priests in the temple profane the Sabbath, and are guiltless? 6 But I tell you that one greater than the temple is here. 7 But if you had known what this means, 'I desire mercy, and not sacrifice,' you would not have condemned the guiltless. 8 For the Son of Man is Lord of the Sabbath." 9 He departed there and went into their synagogue. 10 And behold there was a man with a withered hand. They asked him, "Is it lawful to heal on the Sabbath day?" that they might accuse him. 11 He said to them, "What man is there among you, who has one sheep, and if this one falls into a pit on the Sabbath day, won't he grab on to it, and lift it out? 12 Of how much more value then is a man than a sheep! Therefore it is lawful to do good on the Sabbath day." 13 Then he told the man, "Stretch out your hand." He stretched it out; and it was restored whole, just like the other. 14 But the Pharisees went out, and conspired against him, how they might destroy him.

Compare:
Mark 2:23-3:6
Luke 6:1-11

Notes
1. Tradition said that plucking grain on the Sabbath was an activity forbidden by Exodus 20:8-11.
2. The story of David and his followers is found in 1 Samuel 21:1-6.
3. The Bread of the Presence was baked daily and kept in the Holy place of the Temple.
4. Most rabbis felt that one could attend to accidental injury on the Sabbath, but that ongoing maladies could wait.

Questions for Reflection
1. Now that you are thoughtfully reading this gospel and can see things from Jesus' perspective, do you believe that Christians should observe a Sabbath of complete rest as prescribed by scripture?

2. Do you ever pray about what you could be doing to better observe the Sabbath? Why?

Healing and Power: Matthew 12:15-37 [WEB]

15 Jesus, perceiving that, withdrew from there. Great multitudes followed him; and he healed them all, 16 and commanded them that they should not make him known: 17 that it might be fulfilled which was spoken through Isaiah the prophet, saying, 18 "Behold, my servant whom I have chosen; my beloved in whom my soul is well pleased: I will put my Spirit on him. He will proclaim justice to the nations. 19 He will not strive, nor shout; neither will anyone hear his voice in the streets. 20 He won't break a bruised reed. He won't quench a smoking flax, until he leads justice to victory. 21 In his name, the nations will hope." 22 Then one possessed by a demon, blind and mute, was brought to him and he healed him, so that the blind and mute man both spoke and saw. 23 All the multitudes were amazed, and said, "Can this be the son of David?" 24 But when the Pharisees heard it, they said, "This man does not cast out

demons, except by Beelzebul, the prince of the demons." 25 Knowing their thoughts, Jesus said to them, "Every kingdom divided against itself is brought to desolation, and every city or house divided against itself will not stand. 26 If Satan casts out Satan, he is divided against himself. How then will his kingdom stand? 27 If I by Beelzebul cast out demons, by whom do your children cast them out? Therefore they will be your judges. 28 But if I by the Spirit of God cast out demons, then the Kingdom of God has come upon you. 29 Or how can one enter into the house of the strong man, and plunder his goods, unless he first bind the strong man? Then he will plunder his house. 30 "He who is not with me is against me, and he who doesn't gather with me, scatters. 31 Therefore I tell you, every sin and blasphemy will be forgiven men, but the blasphemy against the Spirit will not be forgiven men. 32 Whoever speaks a word against the Son of Man, it will be forgiven him; but whoever speaks against the Holy Spirit, it will not be forgiven him, neither in this age, nor in that which is to come. 33 "Either make the tree good, and its fruit good, or make the tree corrupt, and its fruit corrupt; for the tree is known by its fruit. 34 You offspring of vipers, how can you pl, being evil, speak good things? For out of the abundance of the heart, the mouth speaks. 35 The good man out of his good treasure brings out good things, and the evil man out of his evil treasure brings out evil things. 36 I tell you that every idle word that men speak, they will give account of it in the day of judgment. 37 For by your words you will be justified, and by your words you will be condemned."

Compare:
Mark 3:7-30
Luke 6:17-19
Luke 11:14-23

Notes
1. The **smoldering wick** [20] in Greek is literally *smoking flax*, idiomatic for a lamp wick whose flame is nearly out.
2. The curing of the inarticulate blind man is described differently in Luke. The miracle can either be portrayed as casting out a demon or curing the victim.
3. The Pharisees, not able to accept Jesus for who He is, attribute His ability to evil forces.
4. Exorcism was widely practiced – not by Jesus alone.
5. The unforgivable sin [31-32] is rooted in total rebellion against God, which isolates that person from God's presence and power.

Questions for Reflection
1. Does Jesus seem to have lost patience with those who cannot accept Him? Why do you think so?

2. What do you think about Jesus' Jewish critics?

3. As a witness to what happened, would you follow Jesus even if you were not one of those who were healed? Why?

Request for a Sign: Matthew 12:38-42 [WEB]

38 Then certain of the scribes and Pharisees answered, "Teacher, we want to see a sign from you." 39 But he answered them, "An evil and adulterous generation seeks after a sign, but no sign will be given it but the sign of Jonah the prophet. 40 For as Jonah was three days and three nights in the belly of the whale, so will the Son of Man be three days and three nights in the heart of the earth. 41 The men of Nineveh will stand up in the judgment with this generation, and will condemn it, for they repented at the preaching of Jonah; and behold, someone greater than Jonah is here. 42 The queen of the south will rise up in the judgment with this generation, and will condemn it, for she came from the ends of the earth to hear the wisdom of Solomon; and behold, someone greater than Solomon is here.

Compare:
Luke 11:29-32

Notes
1. Jeremiah and Ezekiel were among those prophets who described Israel as adulterous because they turned away from God.
2. The **Queen of the South** was undoubtedly the Queen of Sheba as described in 1 Kings 10:1-20.

Questions for Reflection
1. If someone had the reputation for healing, and you witnessed a healing, would that be a sign for you to believe in that person's ability? Why?

2. What credentials does a person need for you to believe that they are sent from God?

3. Are you one who looks for miracles, or do you simply celebrate them when you recognize them? Why?

An Unclean Spirit: Matthew 12:43-45 [WEB]
43 But the unclean spirit, when he is gone out of the man, passes through waterless places, seeking rest, and doesn't find it. 44 Then he says, 'I will return into my house from which I came out,' and when he has come back, he finds it empty, swept, and put in order. 45 Then he goes, and takes with himself seven other spirits more evil than he is, and they enter in and dwell there. The last state of that man becomes worse than the first. Even so will it be also to this evil generation."

Compare: Luke 11:24-26

Note
- Deserts were seen as a favorite place for demons to live.

Questions for Reflection

1. When someone is healed, do they always take steps to try to avoid that affliction in the future?

2. Is preventative medicine only for the body, or for the mind and spirit as well?

Jesus' Real Family: Matthew 12:46-50 [WEB]

46 While he was yet speaking to the multitudes, behold, his mother and his brothers stood outside, seeking to speak to him. 47 One said to him, "Behold, your mother and your brothers stand outside, seeking to speak to you." 48 But he answered him who spoke to him, "Who is my mother? Who are my brothers?" 49 He stretched out his hand towards his disciples, and said, "Behold, my mother and my brothers! 50 For whoever does the will of my Father who is in heaven, he is my brother, and sister, and mother."

Compare:
Mark 3:31-35
Luke 8:4-18

Questions for Reflection

1. Do you think of everyone in your community of faith as brothers and sisters in Christ? Why?

2. Do you treat them like brothers and sisters? How do you do so?

Parable of the Sower: Matthew 13:1-23 [WEB]

1 On that day Jesus went out of the house, and sat by the seaside. 2 Great multitudes gathered to him, so that he entered into a boat, and sat, and all the multitude stood on the beach. 3 He spoke to them many things in parables, saying, "Behold, a farmer went out to sow. 4 As he sowed, some seeds fell by the roadside, and the birds came and devoured them. 5 Others fell on rocky ground, where they didn't have much soil, and immediately they sprang up, because they had no depth of earth. 6 When the sun had risen, they were scorched. Because they had no root, they withered away. 7 Others fell among thorns. The thorns grew up and choked them. 8 Others fell on good soil, and yielded fruit: some one hundred times as much, some sixty, and some thirty. 9 He who has ears to hear, let him hear." 10 The disciples came, and said to him, "Why do you speak to them in parables?" 11 He answered them, "To you it is given to know the mysteries of the Kingdom of Heaven, but it is not given to them. 12 For whoever has, to him will be given, and he will have abundance, but whoever doesn't have, from him will be taken away even that which he has. 13 Therefore I speak to them in parables, because seeing they don't see, and hearing, they don't hear, neither do they understand. 14 In them the prophecy of Isaiah is fulfilled, which says, 'By hearing you will hear, and will in no way understand; Seeing you will see, and will in no way perceive: 15 for this people's heart has grown callous, their ears are dull of hearing, they have closed their eyes; or else perhaps they might perceive with their eyes, hear with their ears, understand with their heart, and should turn again; and I would heal them.' 16 "But blessed are your eyes, for they see; and your ears, for they hear. 17 For most certainly I tell you that many prophets and righteous men desired to see the things which you see, and didn't see them; and to hear the things which you hear, and didn't hear them. 18 "Hear, then, the parable of the farmer. 19 When anyone hears the word of the Kingdom, and doesn't understand it, the evil one comes, and snatches away that which has been sown in his heart. This is what was sown by the roadside. 20 What was sown on the rocky places, this is he who hears the word, and immediately with joy receives it; 21 yet he has no root in himself, but endures for a while. When oppression or persecution arises because of the word, immediately he stumbles. 22 What was sown among the thorns, this is he who hears the word, but the cares of this age and the deceitfulness of riches choke the word, and he becomes unfruitful. 23 What was sown on the good ground, this is he who hears the word, and understands it, who most certainly bears fruit, and brings forth, some one hundred times as much, some sixty, and some thirty."

Compare:
Mark 4:1-20
Luke 8:4-15

Notes
1. A parable is a story told to make a single point. Other than the main lesson in a parable, the details may or may not have bearing on the lesson.
2. The faith of the Disciples enables them to have a deeper understanding of the parables.
3. A parable opens the door to a particular truth. It is up to the hearer whether or not they step through that door with faith in order to see its full meaning.

Questions for Reflection
1. Are some of the seeds of faith wasted by the church as it sows the Word to its community? Why do you think so?

2. Should the church give up when some people do not receive our testimony? Why do you think so?

Parable of the Weeds: Matthew 13:24-30, 36-43 [WEB]

24 He set another parable before them, saying, "The Kingdom of Heaven is like a man who sowed good seed in his field, 25 but while people slept, his enemy came and sowed darnel weeds also among the wheat, and went away. 26 But when the blade sprang up and brought forth fruit, then the darnel weeds appeared also. 27 The servants of the householder came and said to him, 'Sir, didn't you sow good seed in your field? Where did this darnel come from?' 28 "He said to them, 'An enemy has done this.' "The servants asked him, 'Do you want us to go and gather them up?' 29 "But he said, 'No, lest perhaps while you gather up the darnel weeds, you root up the wheat with them. 30 Let both grow together until the harvest, and in the harvest time I will tell the reapers, "First, gather up the darnel weeds, and bind them in bundles to burn them; but gather the wheat into my barn."' …. 36 Then Jesus sent the multitudes away, and went into the house. His disciples came to him, saying, "Explain to us the parable of the darnel weeds of the field." 37 He answered them, "He who sows the good seed is the Son of Man, 38 the field is the world; and the good seed, these are the children of the Kingdom; and the darnel weeds are the children of the evil one. 39 The enemy who sowed them is the devil. The harvest is the end of the age, and the reapers are angels. 40 As therefore the darnel weeds are gathered up and burned with fire; so will it be at the end of this age. 41 The Son of Man will send out his angels, and they will gather out of his Kingdom all things that cause stumbling, and those who do iniquity, 42 and will cast them into the furnace of fire. There will be weeping and the gnashing of teeth. 43 Then the righteous will shine forth like the sun in the Kingdom of their Father. He who has ears to hear, let him hear."

Note
- God allows good to exist in the midst of evil until the time of the harvest – judgment day.

Questions for Reflection
1. Is there a tendency in the church to try to weed out those who have inadequate or wrong beliefs? What have you observed?

2. Is it the church's responsibility to exercise spiritual disciplines within its membership? Why do you think so?

Mustard Seed & Yeast: Matthew 13:31-35 [WEB]

31 He set another parable before them, saying, "The Kingdom of Heaven is like a grain of mustard seed, which a man took, and sowed in his field; 32 which indeed is smaller than all seeds. But when it is grown, it is greater than the herbs, and becomes a tree, so that the birds of the air come and lodge in its branches." 33 He spoke another parable to them. "The Kingdom of Heaven is like yeast, which a woman took, and hid in three measures of meal, until it was all leavened." 34 Jesus spoke all these things in parables to the multitudes; and without a parable, he didn't speak to them, 35 that it might be fulfilled which was spoken through the prophet, saying, I will open my mouth in parables; I will utter things hidden from the foundation of the world."

Compare:
Luke 13:18-21

Treasure, Pearl, and Dragnet: Matthew 13:44-53 [WEB]

44 "Again, the Kingdom of Heaven is like a treasure hidden in the field, which a man found, and hid. In his joy, he goes and sells all that he has, and buys that field. 45 "Again, the Kingdom of Heaven is like a man who is a merchant seeking fine pearls, 46 who having found one pearl of great price, he went and sold all that he had, and bought it. 47 "Again, the Kingdom of Heaven is like a dragnet, that was cast into the sea, and gathered some fish of every kind, 48 which, when it was filled, they drew up on the beach. They sat down, and gathered the good into containers, but the bad they threw away. 49 So will it be in the end of the world. The angels will come forth, and separate the wicked from among the righteous, 50 and will cast them into the furnace of fire. There will be the weeping and the gnashing of teeth." 51 Jesus said to them, "Have you understood all these things?" They answered him, "Yes, Lord." 52 He said to them, "Therefore every scribe who has been made a disciple in the Kingdom of Heaven is like a man who is a householder, who brings out of his treasure new and old things." 53 It happened that when Jesus had finished these parables, he departed from there.

Questions for Reflection

1. Do you find yourself identified in any of these parables? How?

2. Do you believe that any of these parables were hard for His hearers to hear? Why do you think so?

Nazareth Rejection: Matthew 13:54-58 [WEB]

54 Coming into his own country, he taught them in their synagogue, so that they were astonished, and said, "Where did this man get this wisdom, and these mighty works? 55 Isn't this the carpenter's son? Isn't his mother called Mary, and his brothers, James, Joses, Simon, and Judas? 56 Aren't all of his sisters with us? Where then did this man get all of these things?" 57 They were offended by him. But Jesus said to them, "A prophet is not without honor, except in his own country, and in his own house." 58 He didn't do many mighty works there because of their unbelief.

Note

➢ Some scholars use passages like these to argue that Jesus was born in Nazareth.

Questions for Reflection

1. How do you think Jesus felt when some of those who knew Him best rejected Him?

2. Even though Capernaum did not receive Him or His teachings, why might He have used it as His base of operations?

John the Baptist Executed: Matthew 14:1-12 [WEB]

1 At that time, Herod the tetrarch heard the report concerning Jesus, 2 and said to his servants, "This is John the Baptizer. He is risen from the dead. That is why these powers work in him." 3 For Herod had laid hold of John, and bound him, and put him in prison for the sake of Herodias, his brother Philip's wife. 4 For John said to him, "It is not lawful for you to have her." 5 When he would have put him to death, he feared the multitude, because they counted him as a prophet. 6 But when Herod's birthday came, the daughter of Herodias danced among them and pleased Herod. 7 Whereupon he promised with an oath to give her whatever she should ask. 8 She, being prompted by her mother, said, "Give me here on a platter the head of John the Baptizer." 9 The king was grieved, but for the sake of his oaths, and of those who sat at the table with him, he commanded it to be given, 10 and he sent and beheaded John in the prison. 11 His head was brought on a platter, and given to the young lady: and she brought it to her mother. 12 His disciples came, and took the body, and buried it; and they went and told Jesus.

Compare:
Mark 6:14-29
Luke 9:7-9

Notes
1. This Herod was Herod Antipas, who was a son of Herod the Great. This Philip was his half-brother. According to Josephus' *Antiquities*, the daughter's name was Salome.
2. In those times, keeping one's word was more important than right or wrong.

Feeding 5000: Matthew 14:13-21 [WEB]

13 Now when Jesus heard this, he withdrew from there in a boat, to a deserted place apart. When the multitudes heard it, they followed him on foot from the cities. 14 Jesus went out, and he saw a great multitude. He had compassion on them, and healed their sick. 15 When evening had come, his disciples came to him, saying, "This place is deserted, and the hour is already late. Send the multitudes away, that they may go into the villages, and buy themselves food." 16 But Jesus said to them, "They don't need to go away. You give them something to eat." 17 They told him, "We only have here five loaves and two fish." 18 He said, "Bring them here to me." 19 He commanded the multitudes to sit down on the grass; and he took the five loaves and the two fish, and looking up to heaven, he blessed, broke and gave the loaves to the disciples, and the disciples gave to the multitudes. 20 They all ate, and were filled. They took up twelve baskets full of that which remained left over from the broken pieces. 21 Those who ate were about five thousand men, besides women and children.

Compare:
Mark 6:30-44
Luke 9:10-17
John 6:1-13

Note
➢ As was the custom, the women and children sat in an area separated from the men.

Questions for Reflection

1. What is your impression of Jesus' state of mind as He withdraws upon hearing of the death of John?

2. What might be some of the reasons that all four gospel writers tell this story?

Walking on Water: Matthew 14:22-36 [WEB]

22 Immediately Jesus made the disciples get into the boat, and to go ahead of him to the other side, while he sent the multitudes away. 23 After he had sent the multitudes away, he went up into the mountain by himself to pray. When evening had come, he was there alone. 24 But the boat was now in the middle of the sea, distressed by the waves, for the wind was contrary. 25 In the fourth watch of the night, Jesus came to them, walking on the sea. 26 When the disciples saw him walking on the sea, they were troubled, saying, "It's a ghost!" and they cried out for fear. 27 But immediately Jesus spoke to them, saying "Cheer up! It is I! Don't be afraid." 28 Peter answered him and said, "Lord, if it is you, command me to come to you on the waters." 29 He said, "Come!" Peter stepped down from the boat, and walked on the waters to come to Jesus. 30 But when he saw that the wind was strong, he was afraid, and beginning to sink, he cried out, saying, "Lord, save me!" 31 Immediately Jesus stretched out his hand, took hold of him, and said to him, "You of little faith, why did you doubt?" 32 When they got up into the boat, the wind ceased. 33 Those who were in the boat came and worshiped him, saying, "You are truly the Son of God!" 34 When they had crossed over, they came to the land of Gennesaret. 35 When the people of that place recognized him, they sent into all that surrounding region, and brought to him all who were sick, 36 and they begged him that they might just touch the fringe of his garment. As many as touched it were made whole.

Compare:
Mark 6:45-52
John 6:15-21

Notes
1. In the Greek, the boat *was many stadia from the land*. A stadion was about $1/8$ of a mile.
2. The time was the fourth watch of the night, between 3:00 and 6:00 A.M.
3. Gennesaret was a district northwest of the Sea of Gennesaret, also known as the Sea of Tiberias or the Sea of Galilee.

Questions for Reflection
1. Why do you suppose Matthew includes the detail of Peter's venture onto the water, when the other gospel writers do not include it?

2. If you had been in the boat, would you have shared Peter's desire to be with Jesus out on the water? Why?

3. If you had been traveling with Jesus all this time and knew the depths of both His humanity and divinity, how would you have reacted when you saw Jesus on the water? Why?

Tradition & Faithfulness: Matthew 15:1-20 [WEB]

1 Then Pharisees and scribes came to Jesus from Jerusalem, saying, 2 "Why do your disciples disobey the tradition of the elders? For they don't wash their hands when they eat bread." 3 He answered them, "Why do you also disobey the commandment of God because of your tradition? 4 For God commanded, 'Honor your father and your mother,' 'He who speaks evil of father or mother, let him be put to death.' 5 But you say, 'Whoever may tell his father or his mother, "Whatever help you might otherwise have gotten from me is a gift devoted to God,"' 6 he shall not honor his father or mother.' You have made the commandment of God void because of your tradition. 7 You hypocrites! Well did Isaiah prophesy of you, saying, 8 'These people draw near to me with their mouth, and honor me with their lips; but their heart is far from me. 9 And in vain do they worship me, teaching as doctrine rules made by men.'" 10 He summoned the multitude, and said to them, "Hear, and understand. 11 That which enters into the mouth doesn't defile the man; but that which proceeds out of the mouth, this defiles the man." 12 Then the disciples came, and said to him, "Do you know that the Pharisees were offended, when they heard this saying?" 13 But he answered, "Every plant which my heavenly Father didn't plant will be uprooted. 14 Leave them alone. They are blind guides of the blind. If the blind guide the blind, both will fall into a pit." 15 Peter answered him, "Explain the parable to us." 16 So Jesus said, "Do you also still not understand? 17 Don't you understand that whatever goes into the mouth passes into the belly, and then out of the body? 18 But the things which proceed out of the mouth come out of the heart, and they defile the man. 19 For out of the heart come forth evil thoughts, murders, adulteries, sexual sins, thefts, false testimony, and blasphemies. 20 These are the things which defile the man; but to eat with unwashed hands doesn't defile the man."

Compare:
Mark 7:1-23

Notes
1. Traditions were based upon commonly accepted interpretations of the Torah.
2. Ceremonial laws of cleanliness dictate that certain physical conditions can preclude an individual's participation in the community's acts of worship.

Questions for Reflection
1. What are some examples in the Christian community of ritual or tradition having extremely high importance?

2. Describe any habit patterns in your own life that can get in the way when you pursue your relationship with God or with Jesus.

Faith of an Foreigner: Matthew 15:21-28 [WEB]

21 Jesus went out from there, and withdrew into the region of Tyre and Sidon. 22 Behold, a Canaanite woman came out from those borders, and cried, saying, "Have mercy on me, Lord, you son of David! My daughter is severely demonized!" 23 But he answered her not a word. His disciples came and begged him, saying, "Send her away; for she cries after us." 24 But he answered, "I wasn't sent to anyone but the lost sheep of the house of Israel." 25 But she came and worshiped him, saying, "Lord, help me." 26 But he answered, "It is not appropriate to take the children's bread and throw it to the dogs." 27 But she said, "Yes, Lord, but even the dogs eat the crumbs which fall from their masters' table." 28 Then Jesus answered her, "Woman, great is your faith! Be it done to you even as you desire." And her daughter was healed from that hour.

Compare:
Mark 7:24-30

Notes
1. Tyre and Sidon were northwest of His previous location, and were part of the district of Phoenicia.
2. Being from that district, the woman was a Gentile, yet she addresses Him as the Jewish savior.
3. Jesus emphasizes that His primary mission is to call Jews back to God, but He responds to her expression of faith.
4. There are two Greek terms for **dogs**. Jesus uses the term commonly associated with the wild dogs that usually inhabited the refuse heaps outside of established communities. When she responds, she uses the other term in referring to herself, which was usually associated with household pets.

Questions for Reflection
1. Explain how your faith either as simple or as powerful as this woman's.

2. Describe what it would be libe for you to humble yourself to the extent that this woman did.

Another Mass Meal: Matthew 15:29-39 [WEB]
29 Jesus departed there, and came near to the sea of Galilee; and he went up into the mountain, and sat there. 30 Great multitudes came to him, having with them the lame, blind, mute, maimed, and many others, and they put them down at his feet. He healed them, 31 so that the multitude wondered when they saw the mute speaking, injured whole, lame walking, and blind seeing—and they glorified the God of Israel. 32 Jesus summoned his disciples and said, "I have compassion on the multitude, because they continue with me now three days and have nothing to eat. I don't want to send them away fasting, or they might faint on the way." 33 The disciples said to him, "Where should we get so many loaves in a deserted place as to satisfy so great a multitude?" 34 Jesus said to them, "How many loaves do you have?" They said, "Seven, and a few small fish." 35 He commanded the multitude to sit down on the ground; 36 and he took the seven loaves and the fish. He gave thanks and broke them, and gave to the disciples, and the disciples to the multitudes. 37 They all ate, and were filled. They took up seven baskets full of the broken pieces that were left over. 38 Those who ate were four thousand men, besides women and children. 39 Then he sent away the multitudes, got into the boat, and came into the borders of Magdala.

Compare:
Mark 7:31-37, 8:1-10

Question for Reflection
➢ Why is the situation here a bit different from the time Jesus fed the five thousand?

Signs Confrontation: Matthew 16:1-12 [WEB]

1 The Pharisees and Sadducees came, and testing him, asked him to show them a sign from heaven. 2 But he answered them, "When it is evening, you say, 'It will be fair weather, for the sky is red.' 3 In the morning, 'It will be foul weather today, for the sky is red and threatening.' Hypocrites! You know how to discern the appearance of the sky, but you can't discern the signs of the times! 4 An evil and adulterous generation seeks after a sign, and there will be no sign given to it, except the sign of the prophet Jonah." He left them, and departed. 5 The disciples came to the other side and had forgotten to take bread. 6 Jesus said to them, "Take heed and beware of the yeast of the Pharisees and Sadducees." 7 They reasoned among themselves, saying, "We brought no bread." 8 Jesus, perceiving it, said, "Why do you reason among yourselves, you of little faith, 'because you have brought no bread?' 9 Don't you yet perceive, neither remember the five loaves for the five thousand, and how many baskets you took up? 10 Nor the seven loaves for the four thousand, and how many baskets you took up? 11 How is it that you don't perceive that I didn't speak to you concerning bread? But beware of the yeast of the Pharisees and Sadducees." 12 Then they understood that he didn't tell them to beware of the yeast of bread, but of the teaching of the Pharisees and Sadducees.

Compare:
Matthew 11:2-6
Mark 8:11-21
Luke 12:54-56

Note
- The repeated request for a sign may be a concerted effort to catch Jesus contradicting Himself or committing some other error.

Questions for Reflection
1. Why do you think Jesus has to teach the same lessons more than once to His disciples?

2. Why do you suppose the disciples did not understand at first the teaching about yeast and the Pharisees?

Peter's Confession: Matthew 16:13-23 [WEB]

13 Now when Jesus came into the parts of Caesarea Philippi, he asked his disciples, saying, "Who do men say that I, the Son of Man, am?" 14 They said, "Some say John the Baptizer, some, Elijah, and others, Jeremiah, or one of the prophets." 15 He said to them, "But who do you say that I am?" 16 Simon Peter answered, "You are the Christ, the Son of the living God." 17 Jesus answered him, "Blessed are you, Simon Bar Jonah, for flesh and blood has not revealed this to you, but my Father who is in heaven. 18 I also tell you that you are Peter, and on this rock I will build my assembly, and the gates of Hades will not prevail against it. 19 I will give to you the keys of the Kingdom of Heaven, and whatever you bind on earth will have been bound in heaven; and whatever you release on earth will have been released in heaven." 20 Then he commanded the disciples that they should tell no one that he was Jesus the Christ. 21 From that time, Jesus began to show his disciples that he must go to Jerusalem and suffer many things from the elders, chief priests, and scribes, and be killed, and the third day be raised up. 22 Peter took him aside, and began to rebuke him, saying, "Far be it from you, Lord! This will never be done to you." 23 But he turned, and said to Peter, "Get behind me, Satan! You are a stumbling block to me, for you are not setting your mind on the things of God, but on the things of men."

Compare:
Mark 8:27-33
Luke 9:18-22

Notes
1. Jesus clearly means Himself when He says **Son of Man**.
2. The reference to **_flesh and blood_** refers to humanity.
3. Jesus uses a play on words regarding Peter's name. In Greek, *Petros* means Peter and *petra* means rock. In Aramaic, the language Jesus was speaking, the same word was both proper name and a noun. *Kepha* means both.
4. **_Binding_** and **_loosing_** were rabbinical terms referring to forbidding and permitting.
5. **_The Keys to the Kingdom_** are the basis for the church's traditional stand regarding its leadership having descended from Peter to the current Pope.

Questions for Reflection
1. Why is it important for current leaders in the church to be able to make Peter's affirmation without hesitation?

2. Why is it important for all Christians to be able to make this affirmation?

The Cost of Discipleship: Matthew 16:24-28 [WEB]
24 Then Jesus said to his disciples, "If anyone desires to come after me, let him deny himself, and take up his cross, and follow me. 25 For whoever desires to save his life will lose it, and whoever will lose his life for my sake will find it. 26 For what will it profit a man, if he gains the whole world, and forfeits his life? Or what will a man give in exchange for his life? 27 For the Son of Man will come in the glory of his Father with his angels, and then he will render to everyone according to his deeds. 28 Most certainly I tell you, there are some standing here who will in no way taste of death, until they see the Son of Man coming in his Kingdom."

Compare:
Mark 8:34-9:1
Luke 9:23-27

Note
➢ Jesus speaks of life in the larger sense – including the spiritual life and one's total identity.

Question for Reflection
➢ Describe what you feel when it seems as though Jesus has given you too much to handle.

Jesus is Transfigured: Matthew 17:1-8 [WEB]

1 After six days, Jesus took with him Peter, James, and John his brother, and brought them up into a high mountain by themselves. 2 He was transfigured before them. His face shone like the sun, and his garments became as white as the light. 3 Behold, Moses and Elijah appeared to them talking with him. 4 Peter answered, and said to Jesus, "Lord, it is good for us to be here. If you want, let's make three tents here: one for you, one for Moses, and one for Elijah." 5 While he was still speaking, behold, a bright cloud overshadowed them. Behold, a voice came out of the cloud, saying, "This is my beloved Son, in whom I am well pleased. Listen to him." 6 When the disciples heard it, they fell on their faces, and were very afraid. 7 Jesus came and touched them and said, "Get up, and don't be afraid." 8 Lifting up their eyes, they saw no one, except Jesus alone.

Compare:
Mark 9:2-8
Luke 9:28-36

Notes
1. Nearly a week has passed since Peter's confession and affirmation.
2. The mountain was probably Mount Hermon, which is over 9,000 feet in elevation.

Questions for Reflection
1. When Matthew tells this story, what feels different feel about what happened than in the Mark and Luke accounts?

2. If you had been there, how would such a radical change in Jesus' appearance have affected you?

Questions About Elijah: Matthew 17:9-13 [WEB]

9 As they were coming down from the mountain, Jesus commanded them, saying, "Don't tell anyone what you saw, until the Son of Man has risen from the dead." 10 His disciples asked him, saying, "Then why do the scribes say that Elijah must come first?" 11 Jesus answered them, "Elijah indeed comes first, and will restore all things, 12 but I tell you that Elijah has come already, and they didn't recognize him, but did to him whatever they wanted to. Even so the Son of Man will also suffer by them." 13 Then the disciples understood that he spoke to them of John the Baptizer.

Compare:
Mark 9:9-13

Questions for Reflection
1. Have you ever thought about Elijah having a role in the day of judgment? Why?

2. Why do you think the Christian community of today not particularly concerned about the roles of Elijah or John the Baptist in their teaching and preaching?

The Cure of an Epileptic: Matthew 17:14-21 [WEB]

14 When they came to the multitude, a man came to him, kneeling down to him, saying, 15 "Lord, have mercy on my son, for he is epileptic, and suffers grievously; for he often falls into the fire, and often into the water. 16 So I brought him to your disciples, and they could not cure him." 17 Jesus answered, "Faithless and perverse generation! How long will I be with you? How long will I bear with you? Bring him here to me." 18 Jesus rebuked him, the demon went out of him, and the boy was cured from that hour. 19 Then the disciples came to Jesus privately, and said, "Why weren't we able to cast it out?" 20 He said to them, "Because of your unbelief. For most certainly I tell you, if you have faith as a grain of mustard seed, you will tell this mountain, 'Move from here to there,' and it will move; and nothing will be impossible for you. 21 But this kind doesn't go out except by prayer and fasting."

Compare:
Mark 9:14-29
Luke 9:37-42

Notes
1. It was generally thought that epilepsy was caused by demonic forces from the moon.
2. Jesus is not equating *little faith* with lack of belief.
3. Verse 21 is added in a few manuscripts, but scholars consider it a gloss or minor copying variation.

Question for Reflection
➢ Does Jesus seem angry? Why do you think so?

Passion Foretold Again: Matthew 17:22-23 [WEB]

22 While they were staying in Galilee, Jesus said to them, "The Son of Man is about to be delivered up into the hands of men, 23 and they will kill him, and the third day he will be raised up." They were exceedingly sorry.

Compare:
Mark 9:30-32
Luke 9:43-45

Note
➢ The gathering was to organize their trip to Jerusalem for the celebration of the Passover.

Tax Money from a Fish: Matthew 17:24-27 [WEB]

24 When they had come to Capernaum, those who collected the didrachma coins came to Peter, and said, "Doesn't your teacher pay the didrachma?" 25 He said, "Yes." When he came into the house, Jesus anticipated him, saying, "What do you think, Simon? From whom do the kings of the earth receive toll or tribute? From their children, or from strangers?" 26 Peter said to him, "From strangers." Jesus said to him, "Therefore the children are exempt. 27 But, lest

we cause them to stumble, go to the sea, cast a hook, and take up the first fish that comes up. When you have opened its mouth, you will find a stater coin. Take that, and give it to them for me and you."

Notes
1. This passage is unique to Matthew.
2. The temple tax or *didrachma* was a half-shekel in value, and Jewish males paid it for the upkeep of the Temple.
3. The Greek coin was a *stater*, and its value was exactly equal to two *didrachmas*.

Questions for Reflection
1. Have you ever experienced God providing exactly what was necessary to fulfill a need in the church? If so, share your experience.

2. Have you ever experienced God providing what was needed when it was not exactly what you asked for? Describe the difference.

True Greatness: Matthew 18:1-7 [WEB]

1 In that hour the disciples came to Jesus, saying, "Who then is greatest in the Kingdom of Heaven?" 2 Jesus called a little child to himself, and set him in their midst, 3 and said, "Most certainly I tell you, unless you turn, and become as little children, you will in no way enter into the Kingdom of Heaven. 4 Whoever therefore humbles himself as this little child, the same is the greatest in the Kingdom of Heaven. 5 Whoever receives one such little child in my name receives me, 6 but whoever causes one of these little ones who believe in me to stumble, it would be better for him that a huge millstone should be hung around his neck, and that he should be sunk in the depths of the sea. 7 "Woe to the world because of occasions of stumbling! For it must be that the occasions come, but woe to that person through whom the occasion comes! 8 If your hand or your foot causes you to stumble, cut it off, and cast it from you. It is better for you to enter into life maimed or crippled, rather than having two hands or two feet to be cast into the eternal fire.

Compare:
Mark 9:33-37
Luke 9:46-48

Notes
1. Jesus calls for abandoning one's personal goals and simply relating to God as Father.
2. Child-like behavior here simply means recognizing and submitting to the authority of God.

Questions for Reflection
1. How do you distinguish between God's goals for your life and your own?

2. How far are you willing to go in terms of letting God be in charge of your life?

Personal Conduct: Matthew 18:8-9 [WEB]
8 If your hand or your foot causes you to stumble, cut it off, and cast it from you. It is better for you to enter into life maimed or crippled, rather than having two hands or two feet to be cast into the eternal fire. 9 If your eye causes you to stumble, pluck it out, and cast it from you. It is better for you to enter into life with one eye, rather than having two eyes to be cast into the Gehenna of fire.

Compare:
Mark 9:42-48
Luke 17:1-2

Questions for Reflection
1. If all of us are responsible for our own conduct, what about those who blame their behavior on their heredity or genetic makeup? What would you say to them?

2. What about those who blame their environment? What do you say to them?

3. What about those who blame their natural instincts or being human?

The Lost Sheep: Matthew 18:10-14 [WEB]

10 See that you don't despise one of these little ones, for I tell you that in heaven their angels always see the face of my Father who is in heaven. 11 For the Son of Man came to save that which was lost. 12 "What do you think? If a man has one hundred sheep, and one of them goes astray, doesn't he leave the ninety-nine, go to the mountains, and seek that which has gone astray? 13 If he finds it, most certainly I tell you, he rejoices over it more than over the ninety-nine which have not gone astray. 14 Even so it is not the will of your Father who is in heaven that one of these little ones should perish.

Compare:
Luke 15:3-7

Notes
1. Verse 11 is not found in most manuscripts.
2. The reference to **little ones** goes back to the children in the previous discussion.

Church Discipline: Matthew 18:15-20 [WEB]

15 "If your brother sins against you, go, show him his fault between you and him alone. If he listens to you, you have gained back your brother. 16 But if he doesn't listen, take one or two more with you, that at the mouth of two or three witnesses every word may be established. 17 If he refuses to listen to them, tell it to the assembly. If he refuses to hear the assembly also, let him be to you as a Gentile or a tax collector. 18 Most certainly I tell you, whatever things you bind on earth will have been bound in heaven, and whatever things you release on earth will have been released in heaven. 19 Again, assuredly I tell you, that if two of you will agree on earth concerning anything that they will ask, it will be done for them by my Father who is in heaven. 20 For where two or three are gathered together in my name, there I am in their midst."

Compare:
Luke 17:3
Also:
1 Corinthians 6:1-6
James 5:19-20

Notes
1. The phrase **against you** [15] is not in all manuscripts.
2. Discipline of the member when alone [15] is preferred over public embarrassment.
3. Matthew's Jewish male audience, as the maximum expression of rejection, understands the phrase, **Gentile and a Tax Collector**.

Questions for Reflection
1. What are some examples of times when church leaders should exercise discipline among the members?

2. Can you recall an instance when such discipline in the church might have diverted future problems?

Forgiveness Problem: Matthew 18:21-35 [WEB]

21 Then Peter came and said to him, "Lord, how often shall my brother sin against me, and I forgive him? Until seven times?" 22 Jesus said to him, "I don't tell you until seven times, but, until seventy times seven. 23 Therefore the Kingdom of Heaven is like a certain king, who wanted to reconcile accounts with his servants. 24 When he had begun to reconcile, one was brought to him who owed him ten thousand talents. 25 But because he couldn't pay, his lord commanded him to be sold, with his wife, his children, and all that he had, and payment to be made. 26 The servant therefore fell down and kneeled before him, saying, 'Lord, have patience with me, and I will repay you all!' 27 The lord of that servant, being moved with compassion, released him, and forgave him the debt. 28 "But that servant went out, and found one of his fellow servants, who owed him one hundred denarii, and he grabbed him, and took him by the throat, saying, 'Pay me what you owe!' 29 "So his fellow servant fell down at his feet and begged him, saying, 'Have patience with me, and I will repay you!' 30 He would not, but went and cast him into prison, until he should pay back that which was due. 31 So when his fellow servants saw what was done, they were exceedingly sorry, and came and told to their lord all that was done. 32 Then his lord called him in, and said to him, 'You wicked servant! I forgave you all that debt, because you begged me. 33 Shouldn't you also have had mercy on your fellow servant, even as I had mercy on you?' 34 His lord was angry, and delivered him to the tormentors, until he should pay all that was due to him. 35 So my heavenly Father will also do to you, if you don't each forgive your brother from your hearts for his misdeeds."

Notes

1. Forgiveness is not something that can be dealt with like a math problem [22].
2. The Torah provided for selling people for payment of debt.
3. Torture was employed to ascertain whether the person had any hidden assets or wealth.

Questions for Reflection

1. Has there ever been an instance in your life that you felt almost impossible to forgive? If so, describe it.

2. When we fail to forgive, who is the one who is really hurt? Why?

Context of Divorce: Matthew 19:1-12 [WEB]

1 It happened when Jesus had finished these words, he departed from Galilee, and came into the borders of Judea beyond the Jordan. 2 Great multitudes followed him, and he healed them there. 3 Pharisees came to him, testing him, and saying, "Is it lawful for a man to divorce his wife for any reason?" 4 He answered, "Haven't you read that he who made them from the beginning made them male and female, 5 and said, 'For this cause a man shall leave his father and mother, and shall join to his wife; and the two shall become one flesh?' 6 So that they are no more two, but one flesh. What therefore God has joined together, don't let man tear apart." 7 They asked him, "Why then did Moses command us to give her a bill of divorce, and divorce her?" 8 He said to them, "Moses, because of the hardness of your hearts, allowed you to divorce your wives, but from the beginning it has not been so. 9 I tell you that whoever divorces his wife, except for sexual immorality, and marries another, commits adultery; and he who marries her when she is divorced commits adultery." 10 His disciples said to him, "If this is the case of the man with his wife, it is not expedient to marry." 11 But he said to them, "Not all men can receive this saying, but those to whom it is given. 12 For there are eunuchs who were born that way from their mother's womb, and there are eunuchs who were made eunuchs by men; and there are eunuchs who made themselves eunuchs for the Kingdom of Heaven's sake. He who is able to receive it, let him receive it."

Compare:
Mark 10:1-12

Notes
1. Jewish Law does not address the specific question as to lawful cause for divorce. Consequently there were differing opinions on the matter.
2. Jesus' response goes back to God's purpose regarding the marital union.
3. Jesus also recognizes the role of voluntary celibacy in priestly service to God.

Questions for Reflection
1. Why do you think Jesus avoided the temptation of interpreting the law as He was requested?

2. What does Jesus indicate as an overall guiding principles on the subject?

Children Blessed: Matthew 19:13-15 [WEB]

13 Then little children were brought to him, that he should lay his hands on them and pray; and the disciples rebuked them. 14 But Jesus said, "Allow the little children, and don't forbid them to come to me; for the Kingdom of Heaven belongs to ones like these." 15 He laid his hands on them, and departed from there.

Compare:
Mark 10:13-16
Luke 18:15-17

Questions for Reflection

1. Assuming that we are all sinners, and that these children have not been baptized, what is Jesus really saying when He says, " . . . for it is to such as these that the kingdom of heaven belongs?"

2. Do you approach God with a child-like attitude when praying? What does it mean to you?

The Affluent Seeker: Matthew 19:16-30 [WEB]

16 Behold, one came to him and said, "Good teacher, what good thing shall I do, that I may have eternal life?" 17 He said to him, "Why do you call me good? No one is good but one, that is, God. But if you want to enter into life, keep the commandments." 18 He said to him, "Which ones?" Jesus said, "'You shall not murder.' 'You shall not commit adultery.' 'You shall not steal.' 'You shall not offer false testimony.' 19 'Honor your father and mother.' And, 'You shall love your neighbor as yourself.'" 20 The young man said to him, "All these things I have observed from my youth. What do I still lack?" 21 Jesus said to him, "If you want to be perfect, go, sell what you have, and give to the poor, and you will have treasure in heaven; and come, follow me." 22 But when the young man heard the saying, he went away sad, for he was one who had great possessions. 23 Jesus said to his disciples, "Most certainly I say to you, a rich man will enter into the Kingdom of Heaven with difficulty. 24 Again I tell you, it is easier for a camel to go through a needle's eye, than for a rich man to enter into the Kingdom of God." 25 When the disciples heard it, they were exceedingly astonished, saying, "Who then can be saved?" 26 Looking at them, Jesus said, "With men this is impossible, but with God all things are possible." 27 Then Peter answered, "Behold, we have left everything, and followed you. What then will we have?" 28 Jesus said to them, "Most certainly I tell you that you who have followed me, in the regeneration when the Son of Man will sit on the throne of his glory, you also will sit on twelve thrones, judging the twelve tribes of Israel. 29 Everyone who has left houses, or brothers, or sisters, or father, or mother, or wife, or children, or lands, for my name's sake, will receive one hundred times, and will inherit eternal life. 30 But many will be last who are first; and first who are last.

Compare:
Mark 10:17-31
Luke 18:18-30

Notes
1. The young man's question seeks a way of life that Jesus can certify as pleasing to God.
2. Jesus response was typical – suggesting ongoing involvement in the well being of others.
3. God's invitation to eternal life is based upon a humble relationship with God rather than upon ritual.

Questions for Reflection
1. What do you do when your fondness for something or someone comes between you and God?

2. What do you believe is the most important aspect to your relationship with God and/or with Jesus?

Working the Vineyard: Matthew 20:1-16 [WEB]

1 "For the Kingdom of Heaven is like a man who was the master of a household, who went out early in the morning to hire laborers for his vineyard. 2 When he had agreed with the laborers for a denarius a day, he sent them into his vineyard. 3 He went out about the third hour, and saw others standing idle in the marketplace. 4 To them he said, 'You also go into the vineyard, and whatever is right I will give you.' So they went their way. 5 Again he went out about the sixth and the ninth hour, and did likewise. 6 About the eleventh hour he went out, and found others standing idle. He said to them, 'Why do you stand here all day idle?' 7 "They said to him, 'Because no one has hired us.' "He said to them, 'You also go into the vineyard, and you will receive whatever is right.' 8 When evening had come, the lord of the vineyard said to his manager, 'Call the laborers and pay them their wages, beginning from the last to the first.' 9 "When those who were hired at about the eleventh hour came, they each received a denarius. 10 When the first came, they supposed that they would receive more; and they likewise each received a denarius. 11 When they received it, they murmured against the master of the household, 12 saying, 'These last have spent one hour, and you have made them equal to us, who have borne the burden of the day and the scorching heat!' 13 "But he answered one of them, 'Friend, I am doing you no wrong. Didn't you agree with me for a denarius? 14 Take that which is yours, and go your way. It is my desire to give to this last just as much as to you. 15 Isn't it lawful for me to do what I want to with what I own? Or is your eye evil, because I am good?' 16 So the last will be first, and the first last. For many are called, but few are chosen."

Notes
1. Early in the morning means approximately sunrise or 6:00 am.
2. The daily wage would be a Greek denarius. Since smaller coins were available, hourly payment was possible.
3. The owner is willing to be unconventional in practice, and can legally do so as long as the agreement is not violated.

Questions for Reflection
1. Who determines whether or not an agreement with God is being kept?

2. Does God ever fail to keep an agreement or fail to fulfill a promise?

Third Passion Prediction: Matthew 20:17-19 [WEB]

17 As Jesus was going up to Jerusalem, he took the twelve disciples aside, and on the way he said to them, 18 "Behold, we are going up to Jerusalem, and the Son of Man will be delivered to the chief priests and scribes, and they will condemn him to death, 19 and will hand him over to the Gentiles to mock, to scourge, and to crucify; and the third day he will be raised up."

Compare:
Mark 10:32-34
Luke 18:31-34

Note

> The prophecy is very precise in comparison with the other predictions.

Questions for Reflection
1. Why do you think this prophecy is important to Matthew's Jewish audience?

2. Why do you think Jesus is being so concrete and specific this third time?

Honor and Respect: Matthew 20:20-28 [WEB]
20 Then the mother of the sons of Zebedee came to him with her sons, kneeling and asking a certain thing of him. 21 He said to her, "What do you want?" She said to him, "Command that these, my two sons, may sit, one on your right hand, and one on your left hand, in your Kingdom." 22 But Jesus answered, "You don't know what you are asking. Are you able to drink the cup that I am about to drink, and be baptized with the baptism that I am baptized with?" They said to him, "We are able." 23 He said to them, "You will indeed drink my cup, and be baptized with the baptism that I am baptized with, but to sit on my right hand and on my left hand is not mine to give; but it is for whom it has been prepared by my Father." 24 When the ten heard it, they were indignant with the two brothers. 25 But Jesus summoned them, and said, "You know that the rulers of the nations lord it over them, and their great ones exercise authority over them. 26 It shall not be so among you, but whoever desires to become great among you shall be your servant. 27 Whoever desires to be first among you shall be your bondservant, 28 even as the Son of Man came not to be served, but to serve, and to give his life as a ransom for many."

Compare:
Mark 10:35-45
Luke 22:24-27

Questions for Reflection
1. Does one ever gain true honor and respect at the expense of others? Why do you think so?

2. For one to gain honor, where should the initiative come?

3. In the moment of being honored, how does one keep pride under control?

Blind Men at Jericho: Matthew 20:29-34 [WEB]

29 As they went out from Jericho, a great multitude followed him. 30 Behold, two blind men sitting by the road, when they heard that Jesus was passing by, cried out, "Lord, have mercy on us, you son of David!" 31 The multitude rebuked them, telling them that they should be quiet, but they cried out even more, "Lord, have mercy on us, you son of David!" 32 Jesus stood still, and called them, and asked, "What do you want me to do for you?" 33 They told him, "Lord, that our eyes may be opened." 34 Jesus, being moved with compassion, touched their eyes; and immediately their eyes received their sight, and they followed him.

Compare:
Mark 10:46-52
Luke 18:35-43

Notes
1. Jesus seems to not respond to the shout of his title, but responds to the need.
2. Matthew's testimony concerning this episode remembers two blind men rather than one, but does not offer names or heritage as found elsewhere.

Questions for Reflection
1. How is Matthew's testimony different than that of Mark and Luke? [Compare]

2. What details are important for Matthew's Jewish audience?

Triumphal Entry: Matthew 21:1-11 [WEB]

1 When they drew near to Jerusalem, and came to Bethphage, to the Mount of Olives, then Jesus sent two disciples, 2 saying to them, "Go into the village that is opposite you, and immediately you will find a donkey tied, and a colt with her. Untie them, and bring them to me. 3 If anyone says anything to you, you shall say, 'The Lord needs them,' and immediately he will send them." 4 All this was done, that it might be fulfilled which was spoken through the prophet, saying, 5 "Tell the daughter of Zion, behold, your King comes to you, humble, and riding on a donkey, on a colt, the foal of a donkey." 6 The disciples went, and did just as Jesus commanded them, 7 and brought the donkey and the colt, and laid their clothes on them; and he sat on them. 8 A very great multitude spread their clothes on the road. Others cut branches from the trees, and spread them on the road. 9 The multitudes who went before him, and who followed kept shouting, "Hosanna to the son of David! Blessed is he who comes in the name of the Lord! Hosanna in the highest!" 10 When he had come into Jerusalem, all the city was stirred up, saying, "Who is this?" 11 The multitudes said, "This is the prophet, Jesus, from Nazareth of Galilee."

Compare:
Mark 11:1-15
Luke 19:28-38
John 12:12-18

Notes
1. Evidently the animals belonged to a disciple of Jesus.
2. The prophecy refers to Isaiah 62:11 and Zechariah 9:9, but those texts refer to only one animal.
3. The Hebrew exclamation **hosanna** originally was an invocation simply meaning "O Save!" but by the time of Jesus had become an idiomatic expression of joy.

Questions for Reflection
1. Is Palm Sunday an important day of celebration for you? Why?

2. Are there any features to Matthew's account that differ in ways with the other three accounts that you think are important? If so, describe those ways.

Purging the Temple: Matthew 21:12-17 [WEB]

12 Jesus entered into the temple of God, and drove out all of those who sold and bought in the temple, and overthrew the money changers' tables and the seats of those who sold the doves. 13 He said to them, "It is written, 'My house shall be called a house of prayer,' but you have made it a den of robbers!" 14 The blind and the lame came to him in the temple, and he healed them. 15 But when the chief priests and the scribes saw the wonderful things that he did, and the children who were crying in the temple and saying, "Hosanna to the son of David!" they were indignant, 16 and said to him, "Do you hear what these are saying?" Jesus said to them, "Yes. Did you never read, 'Out of the mouth of babes and nursing babies you have perfected praise?'" 17 He left them, and went out of the city to Bethany, and lodged there.

Compare:
Mark 11:11-19
Luke 19:45-48
John 2:13-17

Notes
1. Tradition dictated that only Jewish coins could properly be used in the Temple, hence the need for conversion.
2. The animals were brought in for sacrifice, roasting, and consumption.

Destruction of a Fig Tree: Matthew 21:18-22 [WEB]

18 Now in the morning, as he returned to the city, he was hungry. 19 Seeing a fig tree by the road, he came to it, and found nothing on it but leaves. He said to it, "Let there be no fruit from you forever!" Immediately the fig tree withered away. 20 When the disciples saw it, they marveled, saying, "How did the fig tree immediately wither away?" 21 Jesus answered them, "Most certainly I tell you, if you have faith, and don't doubt, you will not only do what was done to the fig tree, but even if you told this mountain, 'Be taken up and cast into the sea,' it would be done. 22 All things, whatever you ask in prayer, believing, you will receive."

Compare:
Mark 11:12-14, 20-25

Note
➤ In the ancient world, cursing was not seen as sacrilegious behavior but simply as the opposite of a blessing.

Questions for Reflection
1. Did Jesus curse the fig tree to create an opportunity to teach a lesson about faith? What did they learn?

2. Describe the kind of example is Jesus setting here.

Leadership & Authority: Matthew 21:23-32 [WEB]

23 When he had come into the temple, the chief priests and the elders of the people came to him as he was teaching, and said, "By what authority do you do these things? Who gave you this authority?" 24 Jesus answered them, "I also will ask you one question, which if you tell me, I likewise will tell you by what authority I do these things. 25 The baptism of John, where was it from? From heaven or from men?" They reasoned with themselves, saying, "If we say, 'From heaven,' he will ask us, 'Why then did you not believe him?' 26 But if we say, 'From men,' we fear the multitude, for all hold John as a prophet." 27 They answered Jesus, and said, "We don't know." He also said to them, "Neither will I tell you by what authority I do these things. 28 But what do you think? A man had two sons, and he came to the first, and said, 'Son, go work today in my vineyard.' 29 He answered, 'I will not,' but afterward he changed his mind, and went. 30 He came to the second, and said the same thing. He answered, 'I go, sir,' but he didn't go. 31

Which of the two did the will of his father?" They said to him, "The first." Jesus said to them, "Most certainly I tell you that the tax collectors and the prostitutes are entering into the Kingdom of God before you. 32 For John came to you in the way of righteousness, and you didn't believe him, but the tax collectors and the prostitutes believed him. When you saw it, you didn't even repent afterward, that you might believe him.

Compare:
Mark 11:27-33
Luke 20:1-8
John 2:18-22

Notes
1. Temple leaders adhered to strict traditions of behavior, based on the Torah and its interpretation. Their authority came from the Torah and their interpretation of it.
2. John led the life of an ascetic -- austere, modest, and reclusive -- with severe limitations upon pleasures. His authority came from isolation from worldly issues and focus upon God's activity.
3. Jesus led the life of one celebrating the kingdom of God and its gifts, and the offering of God's love. His authority came from the fruits of joy and love.

Questions for Reflection
1. What were the reasons expressed for the Temple leaders' opposition to Jesus' witness?

2. What do you think were the real reasons?

Parable of the Vineyard: Matthew 21:33-46 [WEB]
33 "Hear another parable. There was a man who was a master of a household, who planted a vineyard, set a hedge about it, dug a winepress in it, built a tower, leased it out to farmers, and went into another country. 34 When the season for the fruit drew near, he sent his servants to the farmers, to receive his fruit. 35 The farmers took his servants, beat one, killed another, and stoned another. 36 Again, he sent other servants more than the first: and they treated them the same way. 37 But afterward he sent to them his son, saying, 'They will respect my son.' 38 But the farmers, when they saw the son, said among themselves, 'This is the heir. Come, let's kill him, and seize his inheritance.' 39 So they took him, and threw him out of the vineyard, and killed him. 40 When therefore the lord of the vineyard comes, what will he do to those farmers?" 41 They told him, "He will miserably destroy those miserable men, and will lease out the vineyard to other farmers, who will give him the fruit in its season." 42 Jesus said to them, "Did you never read in the Scriptures, 'The stone which the builders rejected, the same was made the head of the corner. This was from the Lord. It is marvelous in our eyes?' † 43 "Therefore I tell you, the Kingdom of God will be taken away from you, and will be given to a nation bringing forth its fruit. 44 He who falls on this stone will be broken to pieces, but on whomever it will fall, it will scatter him as dust." 45 When the chief priests and the Pharisees heard his parables, they perceived that he spoke about them. 46 When they sought to seize him, they feared the multitudes, because they considered him to be a prophet.

Compare:
Mark 12:1-12
Luke 20:9-19

Note
- The basis for this parable is found in Isaiah 5:1-7.

Questions for Reflection

1. What is the central lesson in this parable?

2. Why do you think is this parable important to Matthew's Jewish audience?

3. Do you think the chief priests saw any truth in the parable? What?

Marriage Feast Parable: Matthew 22:1-14 [WEB]

1 Jesus answered and spoke again in parables to them, saying, 2 "The Kingdom of Heaven is like a certain king, who made a marriage feast for his son, 3 and sent out his servants to call those who were invited to the marriage feast, but they would not come. 4 Again he sent out other servants, saying, 'Tell those who are invited, "Behold, I have prepared my dinner. My cattle and my fatlings are killed, and all things are ready. Come to the marriage feast!"' 5 But they made light of it, and went their ways, one to his own farm, another to his merchandise, 6 and the rest grabbed his servants, and treated them shamefully, and killed them. 7 When the king heard that, he was angry, and sent his armies, destroyed those murderers, and burned their city. 8 "Then he said to his servants, 'The wedding is ready, but those who were invited weren't worthy. 9 Go therefore to the intersections of the highways, and as many as you may find, invite to the marriage feast.' 10 Those servants went out into the highways, and gathered together as many as they found, both bad and good. The wedding was filled with guests. 11 But when the king came in to see the guests, he saw there a man who didn't have on wedding clothing, 12 and he said to him, 'Friend, how did you come in here not wearing wedding clothing?' He was speechless. 13 Then the king said to the servants, 'Bind him hand and foot, take him away, and throw him into the outer darkness; there is where the weeping and grinding of teeth will be.' 14 For many are called, but few chosen."

Compare:
Luke 14:16-24

Notes
1. If Matthew was written in the 80s, the reference to the burning of the city could refer to the destruction of Jerusalem in 70 CE.
2. This parable could be based upon two rabbinical tales. The king invites people to a wedding feast in both without giving a date or time. In one, some put on their wedding robes immediately and wait for the king, while the foolish go on about their work – the moral being centered upon being prepared for the call of God which can come at any time. In the other, some store their robes where they won't get dirty while the foolish others work in their robes, getting them soiled.

Questions for Reflection
1. What is Jesus' request for us to do to be prepared for His call?

2. What are some ways we might live out this parable as Jesus would ask?

The Morality of Taxes: Matthew 22:15-22 [WEB]

15 Then the Pharisees went and took counsel how they might entrap him in his talk. 16 They sent their disciples to him, along with the Herodians, saying, "Teacher, we know that you are honest, and teach the way of God in truth, no matter whom you teach, for you aren't partial to anyone. 17 Tell us therefore, what do you think? Is it lawful to pay taxes to Caesar, or not?" 18 But Jesus perceived their wickedness, and said, "Why do you test me, you hypocrites? 19 Show me the tax money." They brought to him a denarius. 20 He asked them, "Whose is this image and inscription?" 21 They said to him, "Caesar's." Then he said to them, "Give therefore to Caesar the things that are Caesar's, and to God the things that are God's." 22 When they heard it, they marveled, and left him, and went away.

Compare:
Mark 12:13-17
Luke 20:20-26

Note
- The enemies of Jesus thought that with this question they could catch Him in conflict with either religious or secular demands.

Questions for Reflection
1. Is it as important to pay our tithes to the church as it is to pay our taxes? Why?

2. Is it a matter of God needing our money or something else? Be specific.

Resurrection Question: Matthew 22:23-33 [WEB]
23 On that day Sadducees (those who say that there is no resurrection) came to him. They asked him, 24 saying, "Teacher, Moses said, 'If a man dies, having no children, his brother shall marry his wife, and raise up seed for his brother.' 25 Now there were with us seven brothers. The first married and died, and having no seed left his wife to his brother. 26 In the same way, the second also, and the third, to the seventh. 27 After them all, the woman died. 28 In the resurrection therefore, whose wife will she be of the seven? For they all had her." 29 But Jesus answered them, "You are mistaken, not knowing the Scriptures, nor the power of God. 30 For in the resurrection they neither marry, nor are given in marriage, but are like God's angels in heaven. 31 But concerning the resurrection of the dead, haven't you read that which was spoken to you by God, saying, 32 'I am the God of Abraham, and the God of Isaac, and the God of Jacob?' God is not the God of the dead, but of the living." 33 When the multitudes heard it, they were astonished at his teaching.

Compare:
Mark 12:18-27
Luke 20:27-40

Notes
1. In Jesus' time, Pharisees believed in the resurrection, while the Sadducees did not.
2. Jesus points out that lack of belief in the resurrection demonstrates both an ignorance of the scriptures and a fundamental distrust in the power of God.

Questions for Reflection
1. Do you believe in eternal life with God for those who accept Christ? Why?

2. Do you trust in God's ability and willingness to provide eternal life for you?

Greatest Commandment: Matthew 22:34-40 [WEB]
34 But the Pharisees, when they heard that he had silenced the Sadducees, gathered themselves together. 35 One of them, a lawyer, asked him a question, testing him. 36 "Teacher, which is the greatest commandment in the law?" 37 Jesus said to him, "'You shall love the Lord your God with all your heart, with all your soul, and with all your mind.' 38 This is the first and great commandment. 39 A second likewise is this, 'You shall love your neighbor as yourself.' 40 The whole law and the prophets depend on these two commandments."

Compare:
Mark 12:28-34
Luke 10:25-28

Notes
1. In rabbinical schools of that day, asking students to summarize all of the law as briefly as possible was a frequent test.
2. The first part of His answer is part of the *Shema*, the summary creed of Judaism, found in Deuteronomy 6:5. The second is from Leviticus 19:18.

A Question of Ancestry: Matthew 22:41-46 [WEB]
41 Now while the Pharisees were gathered together, Jesus asked them a question, 42 saying, "What do you think of the Christ? Whose son is he?" They said to him, "Of David." 43 He said to them, "How then does David in the Spirit call him Lord, saying, 44 'The Lord said to my Lord, sit on my right hand, until I make your enemies a footstool for your feet?' 45 "If then David calls him Lord, how is he his son?" 46 No one was able to answer him a word, neither did any man dare ask him any more questions from that day forth.

Compare:
Mark 12:35-37
Luke 20:41-44
Also
Psalm 110:1

Notes
1. The initial reference to *Lord* [44] refers to God. It is assumed that the second reference is to the Messiah.
2. Peter picks - this passage in his Pentecost sermon in Acts 2:34-35.

Questions for Reflection
1. While an argument of interest to Jewish Christians, why might Gentiles appreciate this discussion as well?

2. Would this be a good training tool for church attenders?

Contemporary Jewish Leadership: Matthew 23 [WEB]

1 Then Jesus spoke to the multitudes and to his disciples, 2 saying, "The scribes and the Pharisees sat on Moses' seat. 3 All things therefore whatever they tell you to observe, observe and do, but don't do their works; for they say, and don't do. 4 For they bind heavy burdens that are grievous to be borne, and lay them on men's shoulders; but they themselves will not lift a finger to help them. 5 But all their works they do to be seen by men. They make their phylacteries broad, enlarge the fringes of their garments, 6 and love the place of honor at feasts, the best seats in the synagogues, 7 the salutations in the marketplaces, and to be called 'Rabbi, Rabbi' by men. 8 But don't you be called 'Rabbi,' for one is your teacher, the Christ, and all of you are brothers. 9 Call no man on the earth your father, for one is your Father, he who is in heaven. 10 Neither be called masters, for one is your master, the Christ. 11 But he who is greatest among you will be your servant. 12 Whoever exalts himself will be humbled, and whoever humbles himself will be exalted. 13 "Woe to you, scribes and Pharisees, hypocrites! For you devour widows' houses, and as a pretense you make long prayers. Therefore you will receive greater condemnation. 14 "But woe to you, scribes and Pharisees, hypocrites! Because you shut up the Kingdom of Heaven against men; for you don't enter in yourselves, neither do you allow those who are entering in to enter. 15 Woe to you, scribes and Pharisees, hypocrites! For you travel around by sea and land to make one proselyte; and when he becomes one, you make him twice as much of a son of Gehenna as yourselves. 16 "Woe to you, you blind guides, who say, 'Whoever swears by the temple, it is nothing; but whoever swears by the gold of the temple, he is obligated.' 17 You blind fools! For which is greater, the gold, or the temple that sanctifies the gold? 18 'Whoever swears by the altar, it is nothing; but whoever swears by the gift that is on it, he is obligated?' 19 You blind fools! For which is greater, the gift, or the altar that sanctifies the gift? 20 He therefore who swears by the altar, swears by it, and by everything on it. 21 He who swears by the temple, swears by it, and by him who was living in it. 22 He who swears by heaven, swears by the throne of God, and by him who sits on it. 23 "Woe to you, scribes and Pharisees, hypocrites! For you tithe mint, dill, and cumin, and have left undone the weightier matters of the law: justice, mercy, and faith. But you ought to have done these, and not to have left the other undone. 24 You blind guides, who strain out a gnat, and swallow a camel! 25 "Woe to you, scribes and Pharisees, hypocrites! For you clean the outside of the cup and of the platter, but within they are full of extortion and unrighteousness. 26 You blind Pharisee, first clean the inside of the cup and of the platter, that its outside may become clean also. 27 "Woe to you, scribes and Pharisees, hypocrites! For you are like whitened tombs, which outwardly appear beautiful, but inwardly are full of dead men's bones, and of all uncleanness. 28 Even so you also outwardly appear righteous to men, but inwardly you are full of hypocrisy and iniquity. 29 "Woe to you, scribes and Pharisees, hypocrites! For you build the tombs of the prophets, and decorate the tombs of the righteous, 30 and say, 'If we had lived in the days of our fathers, we wouldn't have been partakers with them in the blood of the prophets.' 31 Therefore you testify to yourselves that you are children of those who killed the prophets. 32 Fill up, then, the measure of your fathers. 33 You serpents, you offspring of vipers, how will you escape the judgment of Gehenna? 34 Therefore behold, I send to you prophets, wise men, and scribes. Some of them you will kill and crucify; and some of them you will scourge in your synagogues, and persecute from city to city; 35 that on you may come all the righteous blood shed on the earth, from the blood of righteous Abel to the blood of Zachariah son of Barachiah, whom you killed between the sanctuary and the altar. 36 Most certainly I tell you, all these things will come upon this generation. 37 "Jerusalem, Jerusalem, who kills the prophets, and stones those who are sent to her! How often I would have gathered your children together, even as a hen gathers her chicks under her wings, and you would not! 38 Behold, your house is left to you desolate. 39 For I tell you, you will not see me from now on, until you say, 'Blessed is he who comes in the name of the Lord!'"

Notes

1. This is one of Matthew's extended segments of the teachings of Jesus. Parallel fragments of this chapter are found in the other gospels.
2. The ***phylacteries*** were religious ornamentation consisting of leather containers for the wrists and forehead that contained small scrolls with favorite texts.
3. Tombs were whitewashed before Passover to protect Jewish travelers from accidentally touching them and becoming ceremonially unclean.

4. Scriptures record only one murder of a prophet [2 Chronicles 24:20-22], the prophet Zechariah. Jewish tradition held that others had been killed as well. They were in fact descended from those who killed Zechariah, but Jesus adds that their attitudes are similar.

Questions for Reflection

1. If you can see a contemporary version of the same trap, name it.

2. What can today's church leaders do to avoid falling into a trap like this?

Prediction of Disaster: Matthew 24:1-2 [WEB]

1 Jesus went out from the temple, and was going on his way. His disciples came to him to show him the buildings of the temple. 2 But he answered them, "You see all of these things, don't you? Most certainly I tell you, there will not be left here one stone on another, that will not be thrown down."

Compare:
Mark 13:1-2
Luke 21:5-7

Notes
1. It is assumed by most scholars that the teachings put together by the writer of Matthew for this chapter reflect the events that transpired between 30 and 70 A.D.
2. The discourse that follows, Matthew 24 & 25, is centered on **the end of the age**.

Questions for Reflection
1. When Jesus predicted the destruction of the Temple for the second time, how do you suppose they reacted?

2. How do you react when people want to talk about the "end times?"

Judgement Day: Matthew 24:3-51 [WEB]

3 As he sat on the Mount of Olives, the disciples came to him privately, saying, "Tell us, when will these things be? What is the sign of your coming, and of the end of the age?" 4 Jesus answered them, "Be careful that no one leads you astray. 5 For many will come in my name, saying, 'I am the Christ,' and will lead many astray. 6 You will hear of wars and rumors of wars. See that you aren't troubled, for all this must happen, but the end is not yet. 7 For nation will rise against nation, and kingdom against kingdom; and there will be famines, plagues, and earthquakes in various places. 8 But all these things are the beginning of birth pains. 9 Then they will deliver you up to oppression, and will kill you. You will be hated by all of the nations for my name's sake. 10 Then many will stumble, and will deliver up one another, and will hate one another. 11 Many false prophets will arise, and will lead many astray. 12 Because iniquity will be multiplied, the love of many will grow cold. 13 But he who endures to the end, the same will be saved. 14 This Good News of the Kingdom will be preached in the whole world for a testimony to all the nations, and then the end will come. 15 "When, therefore, you see the abomination of desolation, 1, 2, 3 which was spoken of through Daniel the prophet, standing in the holy place (let the reader understand), 16 then let those who are in Judea flee to the mountains. 17 Let him who is on the housetop not go down to take out things that are in his house. 18 Let him who is in the field not return back to get his clothes. 19 But woe to those who are with child and to nursing mothers in those days! 20 Pray that your flight will not be in the winter, nor on a Sabbath, 21 for then there will be great oppression, such as has not been from the beginning of the world until now, no, nor ever will be. 22 Unless those days had been shortened, no flesh would have been saved. But for the sake of the chosen ones, those days will be shortened. 23 "Then if any man tells you, 'Behold, here is the Christ,' or, 'There,' don't believe it. 24 For there will arise false christs, and false prophets, and they will show great signs and wonders, so as to lead astray, if possible, even the chosen ones. 25 "Behold, I have told you beforehand. 26 If therefore they tell you, 'Behold, he is in the wilderness,' don't go

out; 'Behold, he is in the inner rooms,' don't believe it. 27 For as the lightning flashes from the east, and is seen even to the west, so will be the coming of the Son of Man. 28 For wherever the carcass is, there is where the vultures gather together. 29 But immediately after the oppression of those days, the sun will be darkened, the moon will not give its light, the stars will fall from the sky, and the powers of the heavens will be shaken; 1, 2 30 and then the sign of the Son of Man will appear in the sky. Then all the tribes of the earth will mourn, and they will see the Son of Man coming on the clouds of the sky with power and great glory. 31 He will send out his angels with a great sound of a trumpet, and they will gather together his chosen ones from the four winds, from one end of the sky to the other. 32 "Now from the fig tree learn this parable. When its branch has now become tender, and puts forth its leaves, you know that the summer is near. 33 Even so you also, when you see all these things, know that it is near, even at the doors. 34 Most certainly I tell you, this generation will not pass away, until all these things are accomplished. 35 Heaven and earth will pass away, but my words will not pass away. 36 But no one knows of that day and hour, not even the angels of heaven, † but my Father only. 37 "As the days of Noah were, so will be the coming of the Son of Man. 38 For as in those days which were before the flood they were eating and drinking, marrying and giving in marriage, until the day that Noah entered into the ship, 39 and they didn't know until the flood came, and took them all away, so will be the coming of the Son of Man. 40 Then two men will be in the field: one will be taken and one will be left; 41 two women grinding at the mill, one will be taken and one will be left. 42 Watch therefore, for you don't know in what hour your Lord comes. 43 But know this, that if the master of the house had known in what watch of the night the thief was coming, he would have watched, and would not have allowed his house to be broken into. 44 Therefore also be ready, for in an hour that you don't expect, the Son of Man will come. 45 "Who then is the faithful and wise servant, whom his lord has set over his household, to give them their food in due season? 46 Blessed is that servant whom his lord finds doing so when he comes. 47 Most certainly I tell you that he will set him over all that he has. 48 But if that evil servant should say in his heart, 'My lord is delaying his coming,' 49 and begins to beat his fellow servants, and eat and drink with the drunkards, 50 the lord of that servant will come in a day when he doesn't expect it, and in an hour when he doesn't know it, 51 and will cut him in pieces, and appoint his portion with the hypocrites. There is where the weeping and grinding of teeth will be.

Compare:
Mark 13:3-37
Luke 21:8-36

Notes
1. Jesus seems to be speaking to a wider audience than simply His inner circle.
2. The expression ***this generation*** [34] would idiomatically refer to the people of that time, and would normally refer to a period of 20-30 years since life expectancy was short.

Questions for Reflection
1. Do you think Jesus speaks of the end of the age as being marked by His own passion?

2. Do you think Jesus is juxtaposing images of the end of that age with the end of history or Judgement Day?

Parable of the Bridesmaids: Matthew 25:1-13 [WEB]

1 "Then the Kingdom of Heaven will be like ten virgins, who took their lamps, and went out to meet the bridegroom. 2 Five of them were foolish, and five were wise. 3 Those who were foolish, when they took their lamps, took no oil with them, 4 but the wise took oil in their vessels with their lamps. 5 Now while the bridegroom delayed, they all slumbered and slept. 6 But at midnight there was a cry, 'Behold! The bridegroom is coming! Come out to meet him!' 7 Then all those virgins arose, and trimmed their lamps. 8 The foolish said to the wise, 'Give us some of your oil, for our lamps are going out.' 9 But the wise answered, saying, 'What if there isn't enough for us and you? You go rather to those who sell, and buy for yourselves.' 10 While they went away to buy, the bridegroom came, and those who were ready went in with him to the marriage feast, and the door was shut. 11 Afterward the other virgins also came, saying, 'Lord, Lord, open to us.' 12 But he answered, 'Most certainly I tell you, I don't know you.' 13 Watch therefore, for you don't know the day nor the hour in which the Son of Man is coming.

Notes

1. The parable is about the necessity of being prepared for one's own judgement day.
2. In Palestinian custom, the groom retrieves the bride from her parents' home and takes her to his own.
3. In some manuscripts, the bridesmaids go to meet both the bridegroom and the bride.
4. Literally translated, the ***other bridesmaids*** are virgins.

Questions for Reflection

1. Do you think there is a parallel between the foolish and wise to those who are outside and inside the church? Why?

2. Can you imagine both the foolish and wise types within the church? Why?

Parable of Good Stewardship: Matthew 25:14-30 [WEB]

14 "For it is like a man, going into another country, who called his own servants, and entrusted his goods to them. 15 To one he gave five talents, to another two, to another one; to each according to his own ability. Then he went on his journey. 16 Immediately he who received the five talents went and traded with them, and made another five talents. 17 In the same way, he also who got the two gained another two. 18 But he who received the one went away and dug in the earth, and hid his lord's money. 19 "Now after a long time the lord of those servants came, and reconciled accounts with them. 20 He who received the five talents came and brought another five talents, saying, 'Lord, you delivered to me five talents. Behold, I have gained another five talents besides them.' 21 "His lord said to him, 'Well done, good and faithful servant. You have been faithful over a few things, I will set you over many things. Enter into the joy of your lord.' 22 "He also who got the two talents came and said, 'Lord, you delivered to me two talents. Behold, I have gained another two talents besides them.' 23 "His lord said to him, 'Well done, good and faithful servant. You have been faithful over a few things, I will set you over many things. Enter into the joy of your lord.' 24 "He also who had received the one talent came and said, 'Lord, I knew you that you are a hard man, reaping where you did not sow, and gathering where you did not scatter. 25 I was afraid, and went away and hid your talent in the earth. Behold, you have what is yours.' 26 "But his lord answered him, 'You wicked and slothful servant. You knew that I reap where I didn't sow, and gather where I didn't scatter. 27 You ought therefore to have deposited my money

with the bankers, and at my coming I should have received back my own with interest. 28 Take away therefore the talent from him, and give it to him who has the ten talents. 29 For to everyone who has will be given, and he will have abundance, but from him who doesn't have, even that which he has will be taken away. 30 Throw out the unprofitable servant into the outer darkness, where there will be weeping and gnashing of teeth.'

Compare:
Luke 19:12-27

Note
- A talent was worth more than 15 years' worth of a laborer's standard daily wage.

Questions for Reflection
1. Although the last slave was the worst steward, how would you compare the stewardship of the other two?

2. Are success and profit with the master's investment the only measures of appropriate stewardship? If there are others, specify them.

3. What do you consider the marks of good stewardship for a Christian today?

Parable of the Last Judgment: Matthew 25:31-46 [WEB]
31 "But when the Son of Man comes in his glory, and all the holy angels with him, then he will sit on the throne of his glory. 32 Before him all the nations will be gathered, and he will separate them one from another, as a shepherd separates the sheep from the goats. 33 He will set the sheep on his right hand, but the goats on the left. 34 Then the King will tell those on his right hand, 'Come pl, blessed of my Father, inherit the Kingdom prepared for you from the foundation of the world; 35 for I was hungry, and you gave me food to eat. I was thirsty, and you gave me drink. I was a stranger, and you took me in. 36 I was naked, and you clothed me. I was sick, and you visited me. I was in prison, and you came to me.' 37 "Then the righteous will answer him, saying, 'Lord, when did we see you hungry, and feed you; or thirsty, and give you a drink? 38 When did we see you as a stranger, and take you in; or naked, and clothe you? 39 When did we see you sick, or in prison, and come to you?' 40 "The King will answer them, 'Most certainly I tell you, inasmuch as you did it to one of the least of these my brothers, you did it to me.' 41 Then he will say also to those on the left hand, 'Depart from me, you cursed, into the eternal fire which is prepared for the devil and his angels; 42 for I was hungry, and you didn't give me food to eat; I was thirsty, and you gave me no drink; 43 I was a stranger, and you didn't take me in; naked, and you didn't clothe me; sick, and in prison, and you didn't visit me.' 44 "Then they will also answer, saying, 'Lord, when did we see you hungry, or thirsty, or a stranger, or naked, or sick, or in prison, and didn't help you?' 45 "Then he will answer them, saying, 'Most certainly I tell you, inasmuch as you didn't do it to one of the least of these, you didn't do it to me.' 46 These will go away into eternal punishment, but the righteous into eternal life."

Note:
- This passage has no direct parallel in the other gospels.

Prediction & Conspiracy: Matthew 26:1-5 [WEB]

1 It happened, when Jesus had finished all these words, that he said to his disciples, 2 "You know that after two days the Passover is coming, and the Son of Man will be delivered up to be crucified." 3 Then the chief priests, the scribes, and the elders of the people were gathered together in the court of the high priest, who was called Caiaphas. 4 They took counsel together that they might take Jesus by deceit, and kill him. 5 But they said, "Not during the feast, lest a riot occur among the people."

Compare:
Mark 14:1-2
Luke 22:1-2
John 11:47-53

Notes
1. Caiaphas was the son-in-law of Annas, and was officially appointed high priest by the Roman procurator Valerius Gratus in 26 CE.
2. The term *festival* refers to the entire eight days of celebration of Passover.

Questions for Reflection
1. If you had an unpleasant task to do in the church, would you do it during the Christmas or Easter season? Why?

2. How would you decide whether to wait?

An Act of Devotion: Matthew 26:6-13 [WEB]

6 Now when Jesus was in Bethany, in the house of Simon the leper, 7 a woman came to him having an alabaster jar of very expensive ointment, and she poured it on his head as he sat at the table. 8 But when his disciples saw this, they were indignant, saying, "Why this waste? 9 For this ointment might have been sold for much, and given to the poor." 10 However, knowing this, Jesus said to them, "Why do you trouble the woman? Because she has done a good work for me. 11 For you always have the poor with you; but you don't always have me. 12 For in pouring this ointment on my body, she did it to prepare me for burial. 13 Most certainly I tell you, wherever this Good News is preached in the whole world, what this woman has done will also be spoken of as a memorial of her."

Compare:
Mark 14:3-9
John 12:1-8
Also:
Luke 7:36-50

Notes
1. The name Simon means magician. The identity of this particular Simon is unknown, but he may have been one of those whom Jesus healed – otherwise this would not be taking place in his home.
2. This act leads Jesus to offer praise that is greater than for any other person mentioned in the gospels.

Questions for Reflection
1. Would you feel uncomfortable if a stranger offered this kind of unbidden gracious service to you? Why?

2. Have you ever served a stranger with a gracious and generous act? Why?

Judas Strikes a Bargain: Matthew 26:14-16 [WEB]
14 Then one of the twelve, who was called Judas Iscariot, went to the chief priests, 15 and said, "What are you willing to give me, that I should deliver him to you?" They weighed out for him thirty pieces of silver. 16 From that time he sought opportunity to betray him.

Compare:
Mark 14:10-11
Luke 22:1-2

Note
- The actual value of *thirty pieces of silver* is uncertain since there was more than one kind of silver coin in circulation. Matthew's account refers to the silver shekel. If that was the actual coinage, it was equivalent to about 5,000 [2004 A.D.] American dollars.

Question for Reflection
- Do most Christians betray Jesus in some way at times? If so, give examples.

The Last Supper: Matthew 26:17-29 [WEB]
17 Now on the first day of unleavened bread, the disciples came to Jesus, saying to him, "Where do you want us to prepare for you to eat the Passover?" 18 He said, "Go into the city to a certain person, and tell him, 'The Teacher says, "My time is at hand. I will keep the Passover at your house with my disciples."'" 19 The disciples did as Jesus

commanded them, and they prepared the Passover. 20 Now when evening had come, he was reclining at the table with the twelve disciples. 21 As they were eating, he said, "Most certainly I tell you that one of you will betray me." 22 They were exceedingly sorrowful, and each began to ask him, "It isn't me, is it, Lord?" 23 He answered, "He who dipped his hand with me in the dish, the same will betray me. 24 The Son of Man goes, even as it is written of him, but woe to that man through whom the Son of Man is betrayed! It would be better for that man if he had not been born." 25 Judas, who betrayed him, answered, "It isn't me, is it, Rabbi?" He said to him, "You said it." 26 As they were eating, Jesus took bread, gave thanks for it, and broke it. He gave to the disciples, and said, "Take, eat; this is my body." 27 He took the cup, gave thanks, and gave to them, saying, "All of you drink it, 28 for this is my blood of the new covenant, which is poured out for many for the remission of sins. 29 But I tell you that I will not drink of this fruit of the vine from now on, until that day when I drink it anew with you in my Father's Kingdom."

Compare:
Mark 14:12-25
Luke 22:7-20

Notes
> Jesus' teachings at the table assume the Jewish view of the cosmos. Jews assume that God forgives those who are obedient, that God is savior, and that death is the price of one's sins.

Questions for Reflection
1. Why do you suppose Jesus chose this occasion to announce His betrayal?

2. On this occasion, does Jesus transform the Passover meal, or does he simply add to it?

Warning about Desertion: Matthew 26:30-35 [WEB]
30 When they had sung a hymn, they went out to the Mount of Olives. 31 Then Jesus said to them, "All of you will be made to stumble because of me tonight, for it is written, 'I will strike the shepherd, and the sheep of the flock will be scattered.' 32 But after I am raised up, I will go before you into Galilee." 33 But Peter answered him, "Even if all will be made to stumble because of you, I will never be made to stumble." 34 Jesus said to him, "Most certainly I tell you that tonight, before the rooster crows, you will deny me three times." 35 Peter said to him, "Even if I must die with you, I will not deny you." All of the disciples also said likewise.

Compare:
Mark 14:26-31
Luke 22:31-34
John 13:36-38. 14:31 and 18:1

Notes
1. The *hymn* would be from the second part of the Hallel, all or part of Psalms 115-118.

2. The quotation is from Zechariah 13:7.

Question for Reflection
> Like Peter, have you ever denied being a Christian?

Consecration in Gethsemane: Matthew 26:36-46 [WEB]
36 Then Jesus came with them to a place called Gethsemane, and said to his disciples, "Sit here, while I go there and pray." 37 He took with him Peter and the two sons of Zebedee, and began to be sorrowful and severely troubled. 38 Then he said to them, "My soul is exceedingly sorrowful, even to death. Stay here, and watch with me." 39 He went forward a little, fell on his face, and prayed, saying, "My Father, if it is possible, let this cup pass away from me; nevertheless, not what I desire, but what you desire." 40 He came to the disciples, and found them sleeping, and said to Peter, "What, couldn't you watch with me for one hour? 41 Watch and pray, that you don't enter into temptation. The spirit indeed is willing, but the flesh is weak." 42 Again, a second time he went away, and prayed, saying, "My Father, if this cup can't pass away from me unless I drink it, your desire be done." 43 He came again and found them sleeping, for their eyes were heavy. 44 He left them again, went away, and prayed a third time, saying the same words. 45 Then he came to his disciples, and said to them, "Sleep on now, and take your rest. Behold, the hour is at hand, and the Son of Man is betrayed into the hands of sinners. 46 Arise, let's be going. Behold, he who betrays me is at hand."

Compare:
Mark 14:32-42
Luke 22:40-46
John 18:1

Notes:
1. Literally from the Greek, Jesus says,
   "Spirit . . . intensely sad . . . death . . . abide . . . in this place . . . be vigilant."
2. Jesus is not yearning for death, but He is willing to do God's will – including death.
3. The word that is translated *trial* can also be translated proofing, adversity, or temptation.

Jesus Betrayed by Judas: Matthew 26:47-56 [WEB]
47 While he was still speaking, behold, Judas, one of the twelve, came, and with him a great multitude with swords and clubs, from the chief priest and elders of the people. 48 Now he who betrayed him gave them a sign, saying, "Whoever I kiss, he is the one. Seize him." 49 Immediately he came to Jesus, and said, "Hail, Rabbi!" and kissed him. 50 Jesus said to him, "Friend, why are you here?" Then they came and laid hands on Jesus, and took him. 51 Behold, one of those who were with Jesus stretched out his hand, and drew his sword, and struck the servant of the high priest, and struck off his ear. 52 Then Jesus said to him, "Put your sword back into its place, for all those who take the sword will die by the sword. 53 Or do you think that I couldn't ask my Father, and he would even now send me more than twelve legions of angels? 54 How then would the Scriptures be fulfilled that it must be so?" 55 In that hour Jesus said to the multitudes, "Have you come out as against a robber with swords and clubs to seize me? I sat daily in the temple teaching, and you didn't arrest me. 56 But all this has happened, that the Scriptures of the prophets might be fulfilled."

Compare:
Mark 14:43-52
Luke 22:47-53
John 18:2-12a

Notes
1. The ***crowd*** would seem to indicate that they were expecting organized resistance.
2. Notice that, apart from being present here, only John records Judas' activities during this night.
3. By Roman Army standards, ***twelve legions of angels*** would number more than 72,000.

Questions for Reflection
1. Do you know of any other recorded occasions outside of the Bible where betrayal is with a kiss?

2. What differences do you notice between the gospel accounts of Jesus' arrest?

3. What is important for Matthew and his Jewish audience?

Temple Trial: Matthew 26:57-75 [WEB]

57 Those who had taken Jesus led him away to Caiaphas the high priest, where the scribes and the elders were gathered together. 58 But Peter followed him from a distance, to the court of the high priest, and entered in and sat with the officers, to see the end. 59 Now the chief priests, the elders, and the whole council sought false testimony against Jesus, that they might put him to death; 60 and they found none. Even though many false witnesses came forward, they found none. But at last two false witnesses came forward, 61 and said, "This man said, 'I am able to destroy the temple of God, and to build it in three days.'" 62 The high priest stood up, and said to him, "Have you no answer? What is this that these testify against you?" 63 But Jesus held his peace. The high priest answered him, "I adjure you by the living God, that you tell us whether you are the Christ, the Son of God." 64 Jesus said to him, "You have said it. Nevertheless, I tell you, after this you will see the Son of Man sitting at the right hand of Power, and coming on the clouds of the sky." 65 Then the high priest tore his clothing, saying, "He has spoken blasphemy! Why do we need any more witnesses? Behold, now you have heard his blasphemy. 66 What do you think?" They answered, "He is worthy of death!" 67 Then they spit in his face and beat him with their fists, and some slapped him, 68 saying, "Prophesy to us, you Christ! Who hit you?" 69 Now Peter was sitting outside in the court, and a maid came to him, saying, "You were also with Jesus, the Galilean!" 70 But he denied it before them all, saying, "I don't know what you are talking about." 71 When he had gone out onto the porch, someone else saw him, and said to those who were there, "This man also was with Jesus of Nazareth." 72 Again he denied it with an oath, "I don't know the man." 73 After a little while those who stood by came and said to Peter, "Surely you are also one of them, for your speech makes you known." 74 Then he began to curse and to swear, "I don't know the man!" Immediately the rooster crowed. 75 Peter remembered the word which Jesus had said to him, "Before the rooster crows, you will deny me three times." He went out and wept bitterly.

Compare:
Mark 14:53-72

Luke 22:54-62
John 18:12b-27

Notes
1. The ***Sanhedrin*** is the Jewish supreme court.
2. The demand for Jesus to prophesy [68] indicates that he was blindfolded at this time – an all too common cruel practice used with criminals.
3. Peter was evidently betraying himself with his regional accent. [73]

Questions for Reflection
1. What was the purpose of Jesus' appearing before the Temple authorities?

2. What kind of justice were the Temple authorities seeking?

3. What were the temple authorities actually trying to do?

Jesus Is Sent to Pilate: Matthew 27:1-2 [WEB]

1 Now when morning had come, all the chief priests and the elders of the people took counsel against Jesus to put him to death: 2 and they bound him, and led him away, and delivered him up to Pontius Pilate, the governor.

Compare:
Mark 15:1
Luke 22:66 - 23:2
John 18:28-32

Note
> ➢ This has evidently been a pre-dawn hearing, as Jewish law required formal action by daylight.

Judas Commits Suicide: Matthew 27:3-10 [WEB]

3 Then Judas, who betrayed him, when he saw that Jesus was condemned, felt remorse, and brought back the thirty pieces of silver to the chief priests and elders, 4 saying, "I have sinned in that I betrayed innocent blood." But they said, "What is that to us? You see to it." 5 He threw down the pieces of silver in the sanctuary, and departed. He went away and hanged himself. 6 The chief priests took the pieces of silver, and said, "It's not lawful to put them into the treasury, since it is the price of blood." 7 They took counsel, and bought the potter's field with them, to bury strangers in. 8 Therefore that field was called "The Field of Blood" to this day. 9 Then that which was spoken through Jeremiah the prophet was fulfilled, saying, "They took the thirty pieces of silver, the price of him upon whom a price had been set, whom some of the children of Israel priced, 10 and they gave them for the potter's field, as the Lord commanded me."

Notes
1. This account is unique to Matthew in the gospels.
2. Luke reports the suicide in Acts 1:16-20.
3. Related Hebrew scriptures include Deuteronomy 23:18, Zechariah 11:12-13, and Jeremiah 18:1-3, 32:6-15

Questions for Reflection
1. Have you known a friend or family member who committed suicide? Have you thought about their relationship to God at the time of their death? Share if you are inclined to do so.

2. Do you think that suicide is a sin? Is it unforgivable? Your opinion?

Pilate Questions Jesus: Matthew 27:11-14 [WEB]

11 Now Jesus stood before the governor: and the governor asked him, saying, "Are you the King of the Jews?" Jesus said to him, "So you say." 12 When he was accused by the chief priests and elders, he answered nothing. 13 Then

Pilate said to him, "Don't you hear how many things they testify against you?" 14 He gave him no answer, not even one word, so that the governor marveled greatly.

Compare: Mark 15:2-5
Luke 23:3-4
John 18:33-38

Note
> ➤ The condemned would normally offer a defense, particularly in face of a death penalty, hence Pilate's bewilderment.

Questions for Reflection
1. If you were facing execution because of the exercise of your faith, would you defend yourself? Why?

2. Would you continue to witness to your faith?

The Jesus Barabbas Question: Matthew 27:15-18 [WEB]
15 Now at the feast the governor was accustomed to release to the multitude one prisoner, whom they desired. 16 They had then a notable prisoner, called Barabbas. 17 When therefore they were gathered together, Pilate said to them, "Whom do you want me to release to you? Barabbas, or Jesus, who is called Christ?" 18 For he knew that because of envy they had delivered him up.

Compare:
Mark 15:6-10
John 18:39

Questions for Reflection
1. How do we decide between those traditions that can be justified and those that cannot?

2. Do you believe that the Temple authorities anticipated this response from Pilate?

A Warning: Matthew 27:19 [WEB]
19 While he was sitting on the judgment seat, his wife sent to him, saying, "Have nothing to do with that righteous man, for I have suffered many things this day in a dream because of him."

Note
- This warning is unique to Matthew's gospel, although Luke's gospel [23:4] shows Pilate as seeing the innocence of Jesus.

Questions for Reflection
1. Have you ever awakened with foreboding after a particularly disturbing dream?

2. Have you ever had a dream that turned out to be prophetic? Share it if you feel you can.

The Mob Demands Barabbas: Matthew 27:20-21 [WEB]
20 Now the chief priests and the elders persuaded the multitudes to ask for Barabbas, and destroy Jesus. 21 But the governor answered them, "Which of the two do you want me to release to you?" They said, "Barabbas!"

Compare:
Mark 15:11
Luke 23:18-19
John 18:40

Note
- This point evidently was evidently vitally important to the saga of the early church. Acts 3:13-14 affirms this, which is recorded in all four gospels.

The Mob Demands Crucifixion: Matthew 27:22-23 [WEB]
22 Pilate said to them, "What then shall I do to Jesus, who is called Christ?" They all said to him, "Let him be crucified!" 23 But the governor said, "Why? What evil has he done?" But they cried out exceedingly, saying, "Let him be crucified!"

Compare:
Mark 15:12-14
Luke 23:20-23

Pilate Capitulates: Matthew 27:24-26 [WEB]
24 So when Pilate saw that nothing was being gained, but rather that a disturbance was starting, he took water, and washed his hands before the multitude, saying, "I am innocent of the blood of this righteous person. You see to it." 25 All the people answered, "May his blood be on us, and on our children!" 26 Then he released to them Barabbas, but Jesus he flogged and delivered to be crucified.

Compare:
Mark 15:15
Luke 23:24-25

Notes
1. Matthew is unique in remembering Pilate as washing his hands.
2. Flogging Jesus was a sadistic act of "mercy" – the resulting injuries and pain put Jesus into shock, lessening the pain of crucifixion and hastening Jesus' death.

Jesus Crowned with Thorns: Matthew 27: 27-30 [WEB]
27 Then the governor's soldiers took Jesus into the Praetorium, and gathered the whole garrison together against him. 28 They stripped him, and put a scarlet robe on him. 29 They braided a crown of thorns and put it on his head, and a reed in his right hand; and they kneeled down before him, and mocked him, saying, "Hail, King of the Jews!" 30 They spat on him, and took the reed and struck him on the head.

Compare:
Mark 15:16-19
John 19:1-3

Notes
1. The governor's cohort would probably number about 500 men.
2. Playing games with the accused helped the soldiers deal psychologically with the unpleasant task of execution.

Questions for Reflection
1. Would capital punishment today be as widely accepted if the executioners played with the condemned in this macabre way? Why?

2. By comparison with crucifixion, is today's capital punishment cruel or unusual? Why?

The Death March: Matthew 27:31-32 [WEB]
31 When they had mocked him, they took the robe off of him, and put his clothes on him, and led him away to crucify him. 32 As they came out, they found a man of Cyrene, Simon by name, and they compelled him to go with them, that he might carry his cross.

Compare:
Mark 15:20-22
Luke 23:26
John 19:16b

Notes
1. The procession probably just included Jesus, the other two prisoners, a centurion, and a few other soldiers.
2. Simon of Cyrene was undoubtedly employed because Jesus was both in shock and weak.

The Crucifixion: Matthew 27:33-44 [WEB]
33 They came to a place called "Golgotha," that is to say, "The place of a skull." 34 They gave him sour wine to drink mixed with gall. When he had tasted it, he would not drink. 35 When they had crucified him, they divided his clothing among them, casting lots, 1, 2, 3 36 and they sat and watched him there. 37 They set up over his head the accusation against him written, "THIS IS JESUS, THE KING OF THE JEWS." 38 Then there were two robbers crucified with him, one on his right hand and one on the left. 39 Those who passed by blasphemed him, wagging their heads, 40 and saying, "You who destroy the temple, and build it in three days, save yourself! If you are the Son of God, come down from the cross!" 41 Likewise the chief priests also mocking, with the scribes, the Pharisees, and the elders, said, 42 "He saved others, but he can't save himself. If he is the King of Israel, let him come down from the cross now, and we will believe in him. 43 He trusts in God. Let God deliver him now, if he wants him; for he said, 'I am the Son of God.'" 44 The robbers also who were crucified with him cast on him the same reproach.

Compare:
Mark 15:23-32
Luke 23:32-37
John 19:18-25a

Notes
1. Put to Jesus' lips, the **gall** could have been any bitter liquid.
2. Posting a sign indicating the offense was a widely used custom. Rome recognized the Herod family as having local governmental jurisdiction, so Pilate seems to be labeling Jesus as a pretender to the throne.

Questions for Reflection
1. Ho did the crowd see Jesus – as innocent and sinless? Why?

2. What do you think was the mood of the crowd at this point?

The Death of Jesus: Matthew 27:45-56 [WEB]
45 Now from the sixth hour there was darkness over all the land until the ninth hour. 46 About the ninth hour Jesus cried with a loud voice, saying, "Eli, Eli, lima sabachthani?" That is, "My God, my God, why have you forsaken me?" 47 Some of them who stood there, when they heard it, said, "This man is calling Elijah." 48 Immediately one of them ran, and took a sponge, and filled it with vinegar, and put it on a reed, and gave him a drink. 49 The rest said, "Let him be. Let's see whether Elijah comes to save him." 50 Jesus cried again with a loud voice, and yielded up his spirit.

51 Behold, the veil of the temple was torn in two from the top to the bottom. The earth quaked and the rocks were split. 52 The tombs were opened, and many bodies of the saints who had fallen asleep were raised; 53 and coming out of the tombs after his resurrection, they entered into the holy city and appeared to many. 54 Now the centurion, and those who were with him watching Jesus, when they saw the earthquake, and the things that were done, feared exceedingly, saying, "Truly this was the Son of God." 55 Many women were there watching from afar, who had followed Jesus from Galilee, serving him. 56 Among them were Mary Magdalene, Mary the mother of James and Joses, and the mother of the sons of Zebedee.

Compare:
Mark 15:33-41
Luke 23:44-49
John 19:28-37

Notes
1. When Jesus cried out, he was quoting Psalm 22. Momentarily taking on all the sins of the world our sins blind him to his being able to see God.
2. According to Malachi 4:5-6, Elijah was supposed to usher in the end of history.
3. Offering Jesus vinegar may have been either an attempt to revive Him or to push him deeper into death.

Jesus is Buried: Matthew 27:57-66 [WEB]

57 When evening had come, a rich man from Arimathaea, named Joseph, who himself was also Jesus' disciple came. 58 This man went to Pilate, and asked for Jesus' body. Then Pilate commanded the body to be given up. 59 Joseph took the body, and wrapped it in a clean linen cloth, 60 and laid it in his own new tomb, which he had cut out in the rock, and he rolled a great stone to the door of the tomb, and departed. 61 Mary Magdalene was there, and the other Mary, sitting opposite the tomb. 62 Now on the next day, which was the day after the Preparation Day, the chief priests and the Pharisees were gathered together to Pilate, 63 saying, "Sir, we remember what that deceiver said while he was still alive: 'After three days I will rise again.' 64 Command therefore that the tomb be made secure until the third day, lest perhaps his disciples come at night and steal him away, and tell the people, 'He is risen from the dead;' and the last deception will be worse than the first." 65 Pilate said to them, "You have a guard. Go, make it as secure as you can." 66 So they went with the guard and made the tomb secure, sealing the stone.

Compare:
Mark 15:42-47
Luke 23:50-56
John 19:31-42

Notes
1. Piercing the body was often done to hasten death when it was getting late in the day. Since Jesus was already dead, lymphatic fluid mixed with blood came out.
2. Under normal circumstances, the bodies of those who had been executed were not buried. Often the bodies were left for the birds to pick, and sometimes the bodies were cremated.
3. Joseph of Arimathea is depicted in more Christian art than anyone else except Mary, Joseph, and Jesus.

As It Began to Dawn: Matthew 28:1-10 [WEB]

1 Now after the Sabbath, as it began to dawn on the first day of the week, Mary Magdalene and the other Mary came to see the tomb. 2 Behold, there was a great earthquake, for an angel of the Lord descended from the sky, and came and rolled away the stone from the door, and sat on it. 3 His appearance was like lightning, and his clothing white as snow. 4 For fear of him, the guards shook, and became like dead men. 5 The angel answered the women, "Don't be afraid, for I know that you seek Jesus, who has been crucified. 6 He is not here, for he has risen, just like he said. Come, see the place where the Lord was lying. 7 Go quickly and tell his disciples, 'He has risen from the dead, and behold, he goes before you into Galilee; there you will see him.' Behold, I have told you." 8 They departed quickly from the tomb with fear and great joy, and ran to bring his disciples word. 9 As they went to tell his disciples, behold, Jesus met them, saying, "Rejoice!" They came and took hold of his feet, and worshiped him. 10 Then Jesus said to them, "Don't be afraid. Go tell my brothers that they should go into Galilee, and there they will see me."

Compare:
Mark 16:1-9
Luke 24:1-12
John 20:1-17

Note
- The actual sequence on that first Easter morning is lost to history. Matthew's testimony, addressed to a Jewish audience, reflects his unique condensation of what happened. Read the accounts in the other gospels for comparison

Questions for Reflection

1. As you compare this account with the others, what makes Matthew's account unique?

2. How important is the appearance of the angel to your faith? Would you include it when telling the Easter story without the Bible in front of you? Why?

3. When you tell the story, is it important to you to remember that Jesus said that He would meet His disciples in Galilee? Why?

Dealing with the Guards: Matthew 28:11-15 [WEB]

11 Now while they were going, behold, some of the guards came into the city, and told the chief priests all the things that had happened. 12 When they were assembled with the elders, and had taken counsel, they gave a large amount of silver to the soldiers, 13 saying, "Say that his disciples came by night, and stole him away while we slept. 14 If this

comes to the governor's ears, we will persuade him and make you free of worry." 15 So they took the money and did as they were told. This saying was spread abroad among the Jews, and continues until this day.

Notes
1. Only Matthew includes this detail in his testimony.
2. It would be very risky for soldiers to fabricate a lie. The bribe would have to be large enough both to make sure the soldiers got their stories straight between one another and to insure their sticking together when questioned.
3. It would be likely that the Temple authorities would help the governor back up the soldiers by offering the governor a bribe as well.

Questions for Reflection
1. Why was bribery necessary?

2. If you were one of those who knew the wonderful truth in those days, would you find it difficult to stick to your story? Why?

Commissioning of the Disciples: Matthew 28: 16-20 [WEB]
16 But the eleven disciples went into Galilee, to the mountain where Jesus had sent them. 17 When they saw him, they bowed down to him, but some doubted. 18 Jesus came to them and spoke to them, saying, "All authority has been given to me in heaven and on earth. 19 Go and make disciples of all nations, baptizing them in the name of the Father and of the Son and of the Holy Spirit, 20 teaching them to observe all things that I commanded you. Behold, I am with you always, even to the end of the age." Amen.

Compare:
Mark 16:15-18
John 21
1 Corinthians 15:5-8

Notes
1. The Greek indicates that the disciples prostrated themselves before Jesus [17], which the gospels do not record them doing in any other instance prior to the crucifixion.
2. The formula *in the name* was idiomatic in Hebrew culture to indicate that such was under the protection and power of that name.

Questions for Reflection
1. Does "the Great Commission" have particular meaning or power in your faith experience?

2. Do you feel this commission applies to laity as well as to clergy?

For Further Growth

This workbook emphasizes learning from the Christ of faith depicted in Matthew's Gospel and becoming faithful disciples of Jesus. You have been growing in likeness to Jesus by faithfully following Him, humbly answering questions for reflection, and striving to be like Him. The process is sometimes referred to as sanctification. When Jesus speaks in Matthew's gospel, a person grows closer to him as they learn from him.

Reading other gospels can help you continue your growth. Available on Amazon is a similar workbook entitled ***Encounters with Jesus in John's Gospel***. The approach is identical to the one used in this workbook. The first few pages follow below.

Encounters with Jesus in John's Gospel

A Workbook

by
James J. Stewart

Illustrated by Jenn Kokal

© 2021 James J. Stewart
ISBN: 978-1-7362724-4-2

All Biblical quotations are from:
The World English Bible [WEB]
Derived from the *American Standard Version* ©1901
Published by Rainbow Missions, Public Domain (Copyright waived)

Holiness, like prayer (which is indeed part of it), is something that, though Christians have an instinct for it through their new birth, as we shall see, they have to learn in and through experience.

Packer, J. I., *Rediscovering Holiness* (p. 14). Baker Publishing Group. Kindle Edition.

Table of Contents

Introduction..6
Chapter One 9
Chapter Two...13
Chapter Three..16
Chapter Four 19
Chapter Five...23
Chapter Six...28
Chapter Seven 34
Chapter Eight...41
Chapter Nine 47
Chapter Ten...50
Chapter Eleven 54
Chapter Twelve 59
Chapter Thirteen...65
Chapter Fourteen 71
Chapter Fifteen 78
Chapter Sixteen...82
Chapter Seventeen 86
Chapter Eighteen..89
Chapter Nineteen..94
Chapter Twenty..101
Chapter Twenty-one 105
Other Books by the Author..111

Introduction

As a spiritual and theological way of seeing Jesus, we can think of our Savior as being the human window through whom we see God. The closer we get to a window, the more we see what's beyond the window. Jesus said, "... He who has seen me has seen the Father...." (John 14:9b (WEB)) This statement gives us a glimpse of Jesus' holiness and character.

1 Peter 1:15 [WEB] says, "... but just as he who called you is holy, you yourselves also be holy in all of your behavior...." John's Gospel gives us many examples of Jesus' character and holiness. When we look at these encounters carefully, there is much we can learn. In most instances today, we like our holiness at a distance. Just as surely as we believe in government cutbacks, except in our backyard, we believe in discipline and rigid standards for the other guy, and we believe in mercy for ourselves. Some non-Christians don't want a preacher living next door. When we faithfully follow Jesus and try to be like Him, we should have a good attitude toward holiness. In the original languages of the Bible, holiness refers to being set apart for God, consecrated and surrendered to Him. In a very practical way, to grow towards our savior's holiness means to be a spiritually faithful reflection of Jesus. Encounters with Jesus in John's gospel lead to growth in holiness. We can see it in the apostles, and we can gain it in ourselves.

In the New Testament, there are traditionally four books about the life, death and resurrection of Jesus, our Savior. These four books are located at the start of the New Testament and are known as the Gospels. The word gospel means good news. The New Testament starts with the Gospel of Matthew, followed by that of Mark, Luke, and John. While the Gospels of Matthew, Mark and Luke have numerous parallel passages, the Gospel of John is different. John the Apostle was the youngest of the twelve who were close to Jesus. John's gospel includes fewer accounts of Jesus' public teachings than the gospels of Matthew, Mark, and Luke, but John includes more of what Jesus said in conversations with individuals and small groups. So, there are relatively few direct parallels with the Gospel of John in the other three Gospels. In John, we can observe those closest to Jesus growing towards Jesus' holiness.

John's gospel was written late in the first century after the other gospels were already in circulation. John had no need to reproduce this material, and he chose to write from a more personal point of view. The evidence in the four Gospels indicates that John was remarkably close to Jesus. Maybe it was because John was the youngest and most inexperienced in life, so that Jesus could be especially attentive to always include him in all that happened.

This book sets up encounters with Jesus with a simple approach.

3. Read a few verses of the World English Bible that are provided. (You can also use the version or translation you like best.) Notes are provided in this workbook to aid readers in understanding. Similar notes can be found on Annotated Bibles and Study Bibles.
4. These are followed by questions for reflection, prayer, and discussion. There are not necessarily 'good' or 'bad' answers to these questions. The questions help the reader ponder the character and holiness of Jesus. Some of the questions inspire the faithful disciples of Jesus to think of holiness and to grow towards holiness seen in Jesus.

You do not need to have an extensive knowledge of the Bible or of Jesus to have encounters with Jesus through this book. Small groups can schedule times for discussion by the whole group. As we read the Bible all the time, there is often a way for it to change us. It is because faithfully following Jesus and attempting to be like Him means growing and changing spiritually. While it does not mean achieving Jesus' holiness, it does mean growing towards His holiness and reflecting it as best we can as we faithfully follow Him and try to be like Him. Be sure you use a translation and not a paraphrase, as a modern paraphrase of the Bible is usually not useful for serious study or for spiritual growth.

Chapter One
God's Holiness Descends to Earth in Jesus

 **A Cosmic Vision**

John 1:1-18 [WEB]

1. In the beginning was the Word, and the Word was with God, and the Word was God. 2 The same was in the beginning with God. 3 All things were made through him. Without him, nothing was made that has been made. 4 In him was life, and the life was the light of men. 5 The light shines in the darkness, and the darkness hasn't overcome it. 6 There came a man sent from God, whose name was John. 7 The same came as a witness, that he might testify about the light, that all might believe through him. 8 He was not the light, but was sent that he might testify about the light. 9 The true light that enlightens everyone was coming into the world. 10 He was in the world, and the world was made through him, and the world didn't recognize him. 11 He came to his own, and those who were his own didn't receive him. 12 But as many as received him, to them he gave the right to become God's children, to those who believe in his name: 13 who were born, not of blood, nor of the will of the flesh, nor of the will of man, but of God. 14 The Word became flesh and lived among us. We saw his glory, such glory as of the only born Son of the Father, full of grace and truth. 15 John testified about him. He cried out, saying, "This was he of whom I said, 'He who comes after me has surpassed me, for he was before me.' " 16 From his fullness we all received grace upon grace. 17 For the law was given through Moses. Grace and truth were realized through Jesus Christ. 18 No one has seen God at any time. The only born Son, who is in the bosom of the Father, has declared him.

Notes

1. Instead of starting with the life of Jesus on Earth, the Gospel of John dates back to the beginning of creation, parallel to Genesis.
2. In his gospel, John gives a new meaning to the Greek word, *logos*, which is translated '**word**.' For John and his gospel, that means more than mere words. The word of God is action: to create, transmute, change, and redeem. A direct comparison may be made with the story of creation in Genesis, where, when God speaks, the result is creation itself.
3. In becoming flesh in the person of Jesus, John says that the promises of God (the word of God) are fulfilled.
4. Light was often associated with the truth and wisdom of the Biblical world.
5. With "The Word became flesh and made his dwelling among us," [14] John's original readers received a poignant picture. A literal translation of the Greek can be that He "***pitched tent with us.***"
6. God's grace is now unlimited ["grace upon grace"], as is God's fidelity [truth], and God's intimacy with us [the Father's heart].

Questions for Reflection, Prayer, and Discussion

1. Why is it important to give one's word for something?

2. Since John does not provide a birth story like Matthew and Luke, what does this scripture tell you about the origin of Jesus?

3. Since Jesus is fully God and fully human, what qualities do you expect from him that makes him holy and not just a man?

 **Jesus' Cousin Testifies**

John 1:19-34 [WEB]

19 This is John's testimony, when the Jews sent priests and Levites from Jerusalem to ask him, "Who are you?"

20 He declared, and didn't deny, but he declared, "I am not the Christ."

21 They asked him, "What then? Are you Elijah?"

He said, "I am not."

"Are you the prophet?"

He answered, "No."

22 They said therefore to him, "Who are you? Give us an answer to take back to those who sent us. What do you say about yourself?"

23 He said, "I am the voice of one crying in the wilderness, 'Make straight the way of the Lord,' as Isaiah the prophet said."

24 The ones who had been sent were from the Pharisees. 25 They asked him, "Why then do you baptize if you are not the Christ, nor Elijah, nor the prophet?"

26 John answered them, "I baptize in water, but among you stands one whom you don't know. 27 He is the one who comes after me, who is preferred before me, whose sandal strap I'm not worthy to loosen." 28 These things were done in Bethany beyond the Jordan, where John was baptizing.

29 The next day, he saw Jesus coming to him, and said, "Behold, the Lamb of God, who takes away the sin of the world! 30 This is he of whom I said, 'After me comes a man who is preferred before me, for he was before me.' 31 I didn't know him, but for this reason I came baptizing in water, that he would be revealed to Israel." 32 John testified, saying, "I have seen the Spirit descending like a dove out of heaven, and it remained on him. 33 I didn't recognize him, but he who sent me to baptize in water said to me, 'On whomever you will see the Spirit descending and remaining on him is he who baptizes in the Holy Spirit.' 34 I have seen and have testified that this is the Son of God."

Notes

1. The expectation was that Elijah would return before the arrival of the Messiah. Jesus later attributes that to him.
2. Isaiah, by virtue of his prophecies, was also extensively associated with the coming of the Messiah.
3. Until John the baptist, baptism was associated with conversion to a new religion rather than John's appeal for repentance.

Questions for Reflection, Prayer, and Discussion

1. Between living John's way of life or Jesus' way of life, why does Jesus' way of life appear more attractive?

2. What are some of the benefits of living a life of self-imposed poverty, like John the Baptist lived?

3. When John says that Jesus baptizes with the Holy Spirit, what do you think that means?

READ: The First Followers Encounter Jesus
John 1:35-51 [WEB]

35 Again, the next day, John was standing with two of his disciples, 36 and he looked at Jesus as he walked, and said, "Behold, the Lamb of God!" 37 The two disciples heard him speak, and they followed Jesus. 38 Jesus turned and saw them following, and said to them, "What are you looking for?"

They said to him, "Rabbi" (which is to say, being interpreted, Teacher), "where are you staying?"

39 He said to them, "Come and see."

They came and saw where he was staying, and they stayed with him that day. It was about the tenth hour. 40 One of the two who heard John and followed him was Andrew, Simon Peter's brother. 41 He first found his own brother, Simon, and said to him, "We have found the Messiah!" (which is, being interpreted, Christ). 42 He brought him to Jesus. Jesus looked at him and said, "You are Simon the son of Jonah. You shall be called Cephas" (which is by interpretation, Peter). 43 On the next day, he was determined to go out into Galilee, and he found Philip. Jesus said to him, "Follow me." 44 Now Philip was from Bethsaida, the city of Andrew and Peter. 45 Philip found Nathanael, and said to him, "We have found him of whom Moses in the law and also the prophets, wrote: Jesus of Nazareth, the son of Joseph."

46 Nathanael said to him, "Can any good thing come out of Nazareth?"

Philip said to him, "Come and see."

47 Jesus saw Nathanael coming to him, and said about him, "Behold, an Israelite indeed, in whom is no deceit!"

48 Nathanael said to him, "How do you know me?"

Jesus answered him, "Before Philip called you, when you were under the fig tree, I saw you."

49 Nathanael answered him, "Rabbi, you are the Son of God! You are King of Israel!"

50 Jesus answered him, "Because I told you, 'I saw you underneath the fig tree,' do you believe? You will see greater things than these!"

51 He said to him, "Most certainly, I tell you all, hereafter you will see heaven opened, and the angels of God ascending and descending on the Son of Man."

Notes

1. Philip and Nathaniel appear to experience and respond to the holiness of Jesus.
2. It is generally assumed that Nathaniel is the same person as Bartholomew in the other three Gospels, though this is by no means certain.
3. The name, Peter, means "rock" or "rocky."

Questions for Reflection, Prayer, and Discussion

1. What qualities could Jesus have seen in Peter that caused him to rename him "Rocky?"

2. What "holy" qualities could Nathanael have seen in Jesus who made him abandon all to follow him?

Chapter Two
Christ's Holiness Blesses

 **A Wedding's Miracle Gift**

John 2:1-12 [WEB]

1 The third day, there was a wedding in Cana of Galilee. Jesus' mother was there. 2 Jesus also was invited, with his disciples, to the wedding. 3 When the wine ran out, Jesus' mother said to him, "They have no wine."

4 Jesus said to her, "Woman, what does that have to do with you and me? My hour has not yet come."

5 His mother said to the servants, "Whatever he says to you, do it."

6 Now there were six water pots of stone set there after the Jews' way of purifying, containing two or three metretes apiece. 7 Jesus said to them, "Fill the water pots with water." So they filled them up to the brim. 8 He said to them, "Now draw some out, and take it to the ruler of the feast." So they took it. 9 When the ruler of the feast tasted the water now become wine, and didn't know where it came from (but the servants who had drawn the water knew), the ruler of the feast called the bridegroom

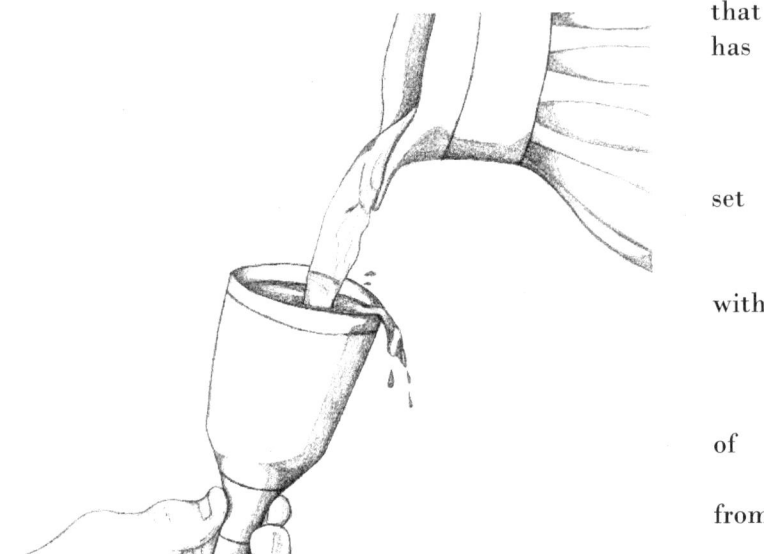

10 and said to him, "Everyone serves the good wine first, and when the guests have drunk freely, then that which is worse. You have kept the good wine until now!" 11 This beginning of his signs Jesus did in Cana of Galilee, and revealed his glory; and his disciples believed in him.

12 After this, he went down to Capernaum, he, and his mother, his brothers, and his disciples; and they stayed there a few days.

Notes

1. Mary knows Jesus' holiness and exercises her knowledge as His mother.
2. Cana is a small village northwest of Nazareth.
3. Jesus' address of Mary translated simply as *woman* was a Greek word used with respect in that culture.
4. Jesus affirms [4] that the time for His being made known as Messiah was to be determined by God – not even by His mother's needs or desires. The celebration may go on for several days.
5. John's term, signs, denotes the events that manifest God's power present in Jesus.

Questions for Reflection, Prayer, and Discussion

1. Although Mary seems to ask her Son a little too much, why do you think Jesus answered as he did?

2. If you were present for this first of His miracles, and recognized it as a miracle, what effect could it have upon you?

3. Do you think the servants who knew the water had been turned into wine may have thought that Jesus was somehow holy?

An Encounter of Righteous Anger
John 2:13-25 [WEB]

13 The Passover of the Jews was at hand, and Jesus went up to Jerusalem. 14 He found in the temple those who sold oxen, sheep, and doves, and the changers of money sitting. 15 He made a whip of cords and drove all out of the temple, both the sheep and the oxen; and he poured out the changers' money and overthrew their tables. 16 To those who sold the doves, he said, "Take these things out of here! Don't make my Father's house a marketplace!" 17 His disciples remembered that it was written, "Zeal for your house will eat me up."

18 The Jews therefore answered him, "What sign do you show us, seeing that you do these things?"

19 Jesus answered them, "Destroy this temple, and in three days I will raise it up."

20 The Jews therefore said, "It took forty-six years to build this temple! Will you raise it up in three days?" 21 But he spoke of the temple of his body. 22 When therefore he was raised from the dead, his disciples remembered that he said this, and they believed the Scripture and the word which Jesus had said.

23 Now when he was in Jerusalem at the Passover, during the feast, many believed in his name, observing his signs which he did. 24 But Jesus didn't entrust himself to them, because he knew everyone, 25 and because he didn't need for anyone to testify concerning man; for he himself knew what was in man.

Notes
1. The temple tax was paid with Jewish money, so Roman currency had to be converted.
2. The animals were utilized for sacrifice.

Questions for Reflection, Prayer, and Discussion
1. Was it a flash of character, or did Jesus express righteousness?

2. Was Jesus out of control?

3. As John was writing his gospel as an old man, do you think he had a full understanding of who Jesus was in terms of being fully human and fully God?

Chapter Three
Holiness is Humbling

READ **A Clandestine Encounter by an Authority:**
John 3:1-21 [WEB]

1 Now there was a man of the Pharisees named Nicodemus, a ruler of the Jews. 2 He came to Jesus by night and said to him, "Rabbi, we know that you are a teacher come from God, for no one can do these signs that you do, unless God is with him."

3 Jesus answered him, "Most certainly I tell you, unless one is born anew, he can't see God's Kingdom."

4 Nicodemus said to him, "How can a man be born when he is old? Can he enter a second time into his mother's womb and be born?"

5 Jesus answered, "Most certainly I tell you, unless one is born of water and Spirit, he can't enter into God's Kingdom. 6 That which is born of the flesh is flesh. That which is born of the Spirit is spirit. 7 Don't marvel that I said to you, 'You must be born anew.' 8 The wind blows where it wants to, and you hear its sound, but don't know where it comes from and where it is going. So is everyone who is born of the Spirit."

9 Nicodemus answered him, "How can these things be?"

10 Jesus answered him, "Are you the teacher of Israel, and don't understand these things? 11 Most certainly I tell you, we speak that which we know and testify of that which we have seen, and you don't receive our witness. 12 If I told you earthly things and you don't believe, how will you believe if I tell you heavenly things? 13 No one has ascended into heaven but he who descended out of heaven, the Son of Man, who is in heaven. 14 As Moses lifted up the serpent in the wilderness, even so must the Son of Man be lifted up, 15 that whoever believes in him should not perish, but have eternal life. 16 For God so loved the world, that he gave his only born Son, that whoever believes in him should not perish, but have eternal life. 17 For God didn't send his Son into the world to judge the world, but that the world should be saved through him. 18 He who believes in him is not judged. He who doesn't believe has been judged already, because he has not believed in the name of the only born Son of God. 19 This is the judgment, that the light has come into the world, and men loved the darkness rather than the light, for their works were evil. 20 For everyone who does evil hates the light and doesn't come to the light, lest his works would be exposed. 21 But he who does the truth comes to the light, that his works may be revealed, that they have been done in God."

Notes

1. The Pharisees were totally devoted to The Torah [law] and to the keeping of it.
2. Rebirth by Baptism was a widely understood concept. When people baptized into Judaism, they even got a new name as a confirmation of their completely new life.
3. The reference to Moses appears in Numbers 21:9.

Questions for Reflection, Prayer, and Discussion

1. What do you say if somebody says they believe they're going to heaven because they're good?

2. When you were baptized, did you emerge from the water with the impression of being a new person?

3. If Nicodemus had at least some sense of the holiness of Jesus, why might Nicodemus think Jesus was different?

Read More Testimony from Jesus' Cousin:
John 3:22-36 [WEB]

22 After these things, Jesus came with his disciples into the land of Judea. He stayed there with them and baptized. 23 John also was baptizing in Enon near Salim, because there was much water there. They came and were baptized; 24 for John was not yet thrown into prison. 25 Therefore a dispute arose on the part of John's disciples with some Jews about purification. 26 They came to John and said to him, "Rabbi, he who was with you beyond the Jordan, to whom you have testified, behold, he baptizes, and everyone is coming to him."

27 John answered, "A man can receive nothing unless it has been given him from heaven. 28 You yourselves testify that I said, 'I am not the Christ,' but, 'I have been sent before him.' 29 He who has the bride is the bridegroom; but the friend of the bridegroom, who stands and hears him, rejoices greatly because of the bridegroom's voice. Therefore my joy is made full. 30 He must increase, but I must decrease.

31 "He who comes from above is above all. He who is from the earth belongs to the earth and speaks of the earth. He who comes from heaven is above all. 32 What he has seen and heard, of that he testifies; and no one receives his witness. 33 He who has received his witness has set his seal to this, that God is true. 34 For he whom God has sent speaks the words of God; for God gives the Spirit without measure. 35 The Father loves the Son, and has given all things into his hand. 36 One who believes in the Son has eternal life, but one who disobeys the Son won't see life, but the wrath of God remains on him."

Notes
1. Purification was a significant ceremonial element in the Jewish religion.
2. Israel is the bride, Jesus the groom, and John is the groomsman.

Questions for Reflection, Prayer, and Discussion
1. As a prophet, do you believe that John knew his cousin well and understood clearly who Jesus was?

2. Why would somebody who heard and saw Jesus return to John with questions?

Chapter Four

Holiness Is Encompassing

An Encounter in Samaria
John 4:1-42 [WEB]

1 Therefore when the Lord knew that the Pharisees had heard that Jesus was making and baptizing more disciples than John 2 (although Jesus himself didn't baptize, but his disciples), 3 he left Judea and departed into Galilee. 4 He needed to pass through Samaria. 5 So he came to a city of Samaria called Sychar, near the parcel of ground that Jacob gave to his son Joseph. 6 Jacob's well was there. Jesus therefore, being tired from his journey, sat down by the well. It was about the sixth hour. 7 A woman of Samaria came to draw water. Jesus said to her, "Give me a drink." 8 For his disciples had gone away into the city to buy food.

9 The Samaritan woman therefore said to him, "How is it that you, being a Jew, ask for a drink from me, a Samaritan woman?" (For Jews have no dealings with Samaritans.)

10 Jesus answered her, "If you knew the gift of God, and who it is who says to you, 'Give me a drink,' you would have asked him, and he would have given you living water."

11 The woman said to him, "Sir, you have nothing to draw with, and the well is deep. So where do you get that living water? 12 Are you greater than our father Jacob, who gave us the well and drank from it himself, as did his children and his livestock?"

13 Jesus answered her, "Everyone who drinks of this water will thirst again, 14 but whoever drinks of the water that I will give him will never thirst again; but the water that I will give him will become in him a well of water springing up to eternal life."

15 The woman said to him, "Sir, give me this water, so that I don't get thirsty, neither come all the way here to draw."

16 Jesus said to her, "Go, call your husband, and come here."

17 The woman answered, "I have no husband."

Jesus said to her, "You said well, 'I have no husband,' 18 for you have had five husbands; and he whom you now have is not your husband. This you have said truly."

19 The woman said to him, "Sir, I perceive that you are a prophet. 20 Our fathers worshiped in this mountain, and you Jews say that in Jerusalem is the place where people ought to worship."

21 Jesus said to her, "Woman, believe me, the hour is coming when neither in this mountain nor in Jerusalem will you worship the Father. 22 You worship that which you don't know. We worship that which we know; for salvation is from the Jews. 23 But the hour comes, and now is, when the true worshipers will worship the Father in spirit and truth, for the Father seeks such to be his worshipers. 24 God is spirit, and those who worship him must worship in spirit and truth."

25 The woman said to him, "I know that Messiah is coming, he who is called Christ. When he has come, he will declare to us all things."

26 Jesus said to her, "I am he, the one who speaks to you."

27 Just then, his disciples came. They marveled that he was speaking with a woman; yet no one said, "What are you looking for?" or, "Why do you speak with her?" 28 So the woman left her water pot, went away into the city, and said to the people, 29 "Come, see a man who told me everything that I have done. Can this be the Christ?" 30 They went out of the city, and were coming to him.

31 In the meanwhile, the disciples urged him, saying, "Rabbi, eat."

32 But he said to them, "I have food to eat that you don't know about."

33 The disciples therefore said to one another, "Has anyone brought him something to eat?"

34 Jesus said to them, "My food is to do the will of him who sent me and to accomplish his work. 35 Don't you say, 'There are yet four months until the harvest?' Behold, I tell you, lift up your eyes and look at the fields, that they are white for harvest already. 36 He who reaps receives wages and gathers fruit to eternal life, that both he who sows and he who reaps may rejoice together. 37 For in this the saying is true, 'One sows, and another reaps.' 38 I sent you to reap that for which you haven't labored. Others have labored, and you have entered into their labor."

39 From that city many of the Samaritans believed in him because of the word of the woman, who testified, "He told me everything that I have done." 40 So when the Samaritans came to him, they begged him to stay with them. He stayed there two days. 41 Many more believed because of his word. 42 They said to the woman, "Now we believe, not because of your speaking; for we have heard for ourselves, and know that this is indeed the Christ, the Savior of the world."

Notes

1. In journeying between Galilee and Judea, it was necessary to pass through Samaria, unless a detour was made by the Jordan.
2. A rabbi rarely spoke with a woman in public, and the Jews thought the Samaritans were outcasts.
3. A prophet was generally considered a person who could settle religious differences.
4. There was a Samaritan temple on Mount Gerizim.

Questions for Reflection, Prayer, and Discussion

1. Why might we think the woman was frightened when she realized that He had intimate knowledge of her life?

2. What was the turning point [if any] for this woman, when she seemed to realize that Jesus was possibly the promised Messiah?

3. What reasons may we have for thinking that this Samaritan is experienced the holiness of Jesus?

 **Return to Galilee**

John 4:43-54 [WEB]

43 After the two days he went out from there and went into Galilee. 44 For Jesus himself testified that a prophet has no honor in his own country. 45 So when he came into Galilee, the Galileans received him, having seen all the things that he did in Jerusalem at the feast, for they also went to the feast. 46 Jesus came therefore again to Cana of Galilee, where he made the water into wine. There was a certain nobleman whose son was sick at Capernaum. 47 When he heard that Jesus had come out of Judea into Galilee, he went to him and begged him that he would come down and heal his son, for he was at the point of death. 48 Jesus therefore said to him, "Unless you see signs and wonders, you will in no way believe."

49 The nobleman said to him, "Sir, come down before my child dies."

50 Jesus said to him, "Go your way. Your son lives." The man believed the word that Jesus spoke to him, and he went his way. 51 As he was going down, his servants met him and reported, saying "Your child lives!" 52 So he inquired of them the hour when he began to get better. They said therefore to him, "Yesterday at the seventh hour, the fever left him." 53 So the father knew that it was at that hour in which Jesus said to him, "Your son lives." He believed, as did his whole house. 54 This is again the second sign that Jesus did, having come out of Judea into Galilee.

Notes

1. The Royal Official suggests someone from King Herod's house.
2. When Jesus speaks of signs and wonders [48], the Greek grammar has **you** in the plural, that is, it is addressed to the whole group.

Questions for Reflection, Prayer, and Discussion

1. Why do you suppose that a *prophet* [44] *has no honor*?

2. Since this is the second sign, what was the first?

3. Can growth towards holiness bring about the glorification of God in this person?

www.ingramcontent.com/pod-product-compliance
Lightning Source LLC
Chambersburg PA
CBHW081357040426
42451CB00018B/3488